COLVILLE

DAVID BURNETT

ART GALLERY OF ONTARIO
McCLELLAND AND STEWART LIMITED
TORONTO

Dog, Boy and St. John River 1958
Oil and synthetic resin on masonite
60.9 x 81.3 cm
London Regional Art Gallery, Ontario
Catalogue Raisonné No. 59

Boat and Marker 1964
Serigraph, edition 17
48.2 x 48.2 cm
Private Collection
Catalogue Raisonné No. 129

Copyright © 1983 Art Gallery of Ontario.
All rights reserved
ISBN: 0-7710-1778-2 paperback
ISBN: 0-7710-1777-4 hardcover

CANADIAN CATALOGUING IN
PUBLICATION DATA

Burnett, David.
Colville

Bibliography: p.
Includes index.

ISBN 0-7710-1778-2 (p.b.)
ISBN-0-7710-1777-4 (bound)

1. Colville, Alex, 1920-   2. Painters-
Canada–Biography. I. Colville, Alex, 1920-
II. Art Gallery of Ontario. III Title.

ND249.C55B87 1983   759.11
C83-094112-6

The Art Gallery of Ontario is funded by the Province of Ontario, the Ministry of Citizenship and Culture, the Municipality of Metropolitan Toronto, and the Government of Canada through the National Museums Corporation and the Canada Council.

Design: Ivan Holmes, Art Gallery of Ontario

PHOTO CREDITS

Numbers indicated below are Catalogue Raisonné numbers.

Art Gallery of Ontario, Larry Ostrom: 16, 18, 38, 39, 42, 52, 59, 80, 86, 88, 89, 91, 111, 132, 133, 137, 138, 139, 141; Courtesy Beaverbrook Art Gallery: 19, 24; H. and V.v. Brauchitsch: 106; Centre national d'art et de culture Georges Pompidou: 82; James A. Chambers: 11, 14, 26, 27, 32, 37, 41, 43, 51, 54, 57, 60, 61, 67, 70, 73, 83, 90, 109, 112, 113, 129; Fischer Fine Art, London: 85; Foto Mayr: 87; Courtesy Hallmark Cards Inc.: 50; David Hawkins, Sackville: 35; Hill Photography: 68; Robert Keziere: 108; Courtesy Kitchener-Waterloo Art Gallery: 84; Courtesy MacDonald Stewart Art Centre: 46; Manfred Rischer, Düsseldorf: 81; G. Mangold: 79; Mendel Art Gallery: 44; The Montreal Museum of Fine Arts: 71; The Museum of Modern Art, New York: 72; National Gallery of Canada, Ottawa: 29, 30, 34, 49, 53, 55, 56, 58, 74; Art Bank of Nova Scotia: 21; Eric Pollitzer Ltd.: 65; Pridham's Studio Ltd., Barry MacKay: 63; Prudence Cuming Assoc. Ltd.: 69, 107, 114, 115, 116, 117, 118, 119, 140, 142, 143, 144; Staatliche Museen zu Berlin: 110; Station House Studio, New Brunswick: 22; Studio Service Bonn: 75; Tischer Foto: 76; University of California, Santa Cruz: 77.

On the Cover:
Target Pistol and Man 1980
Acrylic polymer emulsion
60 x 60 cm
Private Collection
Detail on front cover; complete work on back cover.

Printed in Hong Kong
by Everbest Printing Co., Ltd.

Photograph of Alex Colville (frontispiece)
by Arnaud Maggs.

CONTENTS

January

February

March

July

August

September

Labours of the Months 1978
Boxed set of 12 lithographs
20.0 x 20.0 cm each
Mira Godard Gallery
Catalogue Raisonné No. 141

April

May

June

October

November

December

PREFACE

This book marks in two ways an event that the Art Gallery of Ontario takes much pleasure in presenting. It records the first retrospective of the work of Alex Colville and, as a publishing venture, seeks to extend a knowledge and appreciation of his work beyond the occasion of the exhibition.

Colville's name is a familiar one to Canadians; his reputation is firmly established and his work widely respected. But although his work has often been shown in Canada and Europe, this exhibition is the first to give a substantial overview of his career from the war years to the present. Few of his paintings of the past twenty years have found their way into public collections, so that it is a rare opportunity to assess his remarkable contribution.

By co-publishing this book with McClelland and Stewart, the Art Gallery of Ontario is able to present not only a record of the exhibition but also a monograph on Colville's entire career. The book, written by David Burnett, Curator of Contemporary Canadian Art, who was also responsible for organizing the exhibition, marks an important addition to the growing list of publications on Canadian art.

We anticipate that the exhibition will generate a great deal of interest and give much pleasure to the audiences who will see it in Canada and Germany. This book will enhance their enjoyment and open Colville's work to an even wider public. For both these reasons we have welcomed the opportunity to present the achievements of one of Canada's major artistic figures.

William J. Withrow

Director
Art Gallery of Ontario

Windmill and Farm 1947
Oil on masonite
71.1 x 55.9 cm
Collection Dr. Elizabeth Harfenist
Catalogue Raisonné No. 18

ACKNOWLEDGEMENTS

It was with great anticipation but some concern that I first travelled to Wolfville to meet Alex Colville. To present the work of a living artist is a special responsibility that must rest on a relationship of openness and trust between artist and curator. Any concern I had was immediately dissolved by the warmth with which Alex and Rhoda welcomed me to their home; I was made to feel as though I had known them for years. My subsequent visits have built on that first experience and it has made the preparation of the exhibition and the book the most pleasurable work that I have ever undertaken. My first thanks go, quite naturally, to Alex and Rhoda for their hospitality, their help, their patience, and their friendship.

In building an exhibition of an artist of Colville's stature, the key element is not so much in choosing the works as in obtaining the loans. His paintings are widely scattered in public and private collections and each of them, because of their rarity, holds a special place in any collection – there are no substitutes. I have been met, in approaching owners, with almost universal agreement to lend their paintings to the exhibition. I know how difficult this has been for many people and I have been impressed by their generosity, their deep regard for Alex Colville, and their sincere pleasure in being able to share their special possessions with others. My thanks go to all those lenders for making this exhibition possible.

Within the Art Gallery of Ontario many people have worked very hard to make this exhibition a success. The size and complexity of the catalogue has made special demands on Denise Bukowski, Head of Publications, Ivan Holmes, Designer, Catherine Van Baren, Production Editor, and Maia Sutnik, Head of Photographic Services. The success of the finished product is due in large measure to their tireless efforts. Barry Simpson, Manager of Exhibitions, and Mara Meikle, my secretary, have coped calmly and efficiently with the hundreds of details that go into making a major exhibition. My thanks also to Eva Robinson, Registrar, Ches Taylor, Head of Technical Services, and John Rusekas, Chief Preparator. I am grateful to Roald Nasgaard for reading my text in draft form. My special and personal debt is to Marilyn Schiff, who compiled the catalogue raisonné and bibliography, read and corrected the text in all its drafts, typed most of them, and gave me all the support anyone can hope to expect.

David Burnett

It seems right that the exhibition that this book records should open in Toronto, where I spent my first seven years. I remember seeing *All Quiet on the Western Front* (the early, silent version), I think, in a theatre on St. Clair Avenue in the pre-babysitter era about 1925. Ten years later, when visiting Toronto with my mother, I made my first of many visits to museums when her father, a tailor with a meditative mind, took me to the Royal Ontario Museum, where I saw ancient Egyptian art including a mummy.

Recently I was talking at a dinner with a young man who had just won a Rhodes scholarship. He had studied philosophy, and I observed that I liked Nietzsche's idea of *Amor Fati* – the love of fate. After a pause, he said that perhaps I had more reason to love fate than most people. It is true that I have enjoyed extraordinary liberty and independence. My parents, who were not well off, supported my decision made in Amherst, Nova Scotia, in 1938 to become an artist. My teacher, the late Stanley Royle, gave me free rein, but helped when I wanted it. When I was a war artist I experienced not rejection, but the touching regard that soldiers have for someone who is recording their (often brief) lives. Later, I benefited from the "I-and-thou" relationship with students. When I began to mature as an artist, at about age thirty, I was doing work that was then unfashionable, but I received support and encouragement (extremely valuable to me at that time) from a few people. These included Avery Shaw, art curator of the New Brunswick Museum until his death in 1956, Bob Hubbard, then of the National Gallery of Canada, and Lincoln Kirstein in New York. Much later I enjoyed the friendship and entrepreneurial skill of the late Harry Fischer of London. My wife and I met as students and have been married for forty years; my life and work owe much to this union. I have vicariously experienced the lives of numerous animals; some living, some in animal heaven – there is no limbo, purgatory, or hell for animals.

Now my work is honoured by being assembled and shown at the Art Gallery of Ontario and other institutions in Germany and Canada. Almost everything has been loaned from public and private collections; I am grateful to the boards and the individuals who have been so generous, and to the various agencies that have borne the cost of this project. I appreciate the close and ruminative attention that David Burnett has given to my work.

Last year I was looking at Titian's *Death of Acteon* in the National Gallery in London. It is thought that he painted this affecting work in his nineties. I like to think that I may have another thirty years of work ahead of me.

Alex Colville

December 28, 1982

Target Pistol and Man 1980
Acrylic polymer emulsion
60.0 x 60.0 cm
Private Collection
Catalogue Raisonné No. 117

ONE

THE ART OF ALEX COLVILLE

The art of Alex Colville, already fully formed in the 1950s, stood for a long time as an isolated phenomenon. Its very popularity seemed to militate against its seriousness. Colville wrote about this issue in 1973, at a time when his reputation was widely and firmly established:

> Perhaps the most remarkable feature of my paintings is that they are, to an extent unusual in the art of this century, "popular"; they do not belong exclusively to the art world....
>
> But if one is not to accept the argument that my work is rather popular because it is bad (commercial, sentimental, retrogressive) then one is asserting that it is perhaps good, *although* popular. Then the question is: can this be possible? – and if it can be, how does one explain it? I am inclined to think that this is the central issue in considering my work.

The answers to these questions were, in his own mind, to be found by facing the fundamental issues in his life and by expressing them in painting:

> I do not find life boring or banal. Consequently I am not in flight from what might be called ordinary experience. Hannah Arendt has written of the banality of evil; I once said that I painted persons, animals, situations which I considered wholly good...[by which] I mean not banal.... But as soon as one speaks of banality... then of evil, then of good, one is moving, perhaps involuntarily, from the realm of esthetics into the realm of the moral.... One of my basic convictions is that art and morality have a necessary, though tense and ambiguous relationship.[1]

At the core of Colville's work is the fact that he represents his individual experience; he responds through his art to the world he knows in his daily life. He does not simply record what he sees (or would like to see), but brings his values, his relationships, and his memories to a concrete and immediate synthesis. To illustrate this distinction he has compared photography and painting, the difference between the way a photograph is "taken" and a painting is "made."[2] Each of his works is not a slice of the world, but a unique visual image collected from his experience, his memory, and his imagination.

Such an image depends on a long and thoughtful preparation involving an exhaustive series of drawings and a meticulous painting technique. He may carry an idea with him for five or ten years or more before transforming it into a painting. During this period he may work on the idea from time to time in drawings, and then leave it – "withhold," as he says – until the precise moment for working on the painting is right. When he begins the process of making a painting it absorbs all his attention. He works on just one piece at a time, completing that, no matter what difficulties it presents him, before turning to something new.

The objective procedure of making the pictures must be underlined if we are to look at Colville's paintings with more than an admiration for their precision or a fascination with the sense of unease they may give us. We must look very closely at them; a glance reveals only a reflection, a related but insubstantial form. Each picture constructs its own space and moment of time from the viewpoint of the artist; but each one is always open in a precise way to the spectator, a way similar to the young Martin Buber's notion, following Kant, that the mysteries of time and space were constructions of the human mind, and that what really confronted him in them was the mystery of his own being.[3] In Colville's work the mystery is not some secret hidden within an image, but the revelation of his own understanding of people, animals, places, and himself. And our reception of the paintings opens that mystery into our own. This is, for Colville, the essence of communication:

> If [the artist's] attention to the continuous buzz and flicker of experience and his struggle to transmit these into forms results in an authentic work, other people will experience from it a kind of ordering, fulfilling, illuminating sensation.[4]

When he says that his work does not belong exclusively to the art world he means, in part, that he seeks to address in it questions that are philosophic rather than artistic:

> There *are* these basic questions: "What's it all about?"; "What's happening?"; "What is life like?" Of course there are no specific answers to these questions, perhaps no answers at all, but people who work with this sort of question in mind do tend, I suggest, to produce work which is interesting to some people who do not have a special interest in the visual arts. In a sense, we are discussing here some characteristics of an essentially unsophisticated, that is to say, primitive art.
>
> For a painter with this sort of preoccupation, the contemporary art world is not very interesting....[5]

It may seem strange to find Colville describing his art as "primitive." What he means is that his concern is with the "questions without answer" and that he must go to these directly, not through a critical base of other art. His interest in other painting, at least as he has felt it related to his own work, has always been highly selective.

In many respects the most significant development of his intellectual interests came through his love of literature. He has read and continues to read avidly from a wide range of writing, in poetry and philosophy, but above all, in modern fiction. It has had a profound effect on his approach to painting, in two ways particularly. First, the communication of ideas through the viewpoints in his pictures parallels the fictional devices by which the author expresses his ideas and addresses the reader. This methodology is given form in a number of ways in Colville's work, not least of which is the frequent inclusion of himself in his pictures, drawing the spectator to identify his own place with the artist's in an interchange of subjectivities. Even in those pictures where he does not include himself, the precision with which the painting is constructed puts the spectator directly in the artist's place, as if he had just stepped aside to allow us to take over his position.

The second way in which the example of literature has played a crucial part in Colville's approach to his painting is in his use of metaphor. With relatively few exceptions he avoids the traditional iconography of painting and allows the naturalistic elements of a picture to serve both as description and as symbol. In this way every element within a picture is interwoven among several layers of significance. His images are always fictions, constructions formed from the complex of his experience.

The parallel with literature carries one major *caveat*, however. His paintings are not sections of a narrative. The picture we have before us is the whole of its meaning, rather than one moment for which we must reconstruct the prior and succeeding moments. The essence of a painting lies in its construction of space.

The origin of a particular subject is for Colville always an intuitive response to something he sees. This could be the pose of a figure, a setting, a simple everyday activity–something that catches his attention and interest without his knowing why, or how he might use it. It is, he says, similar to Nabokov's description of beginning to write a novel with "only the shadow of an object that is not yet present."[6] For Colville it may be months or years before this "shadow" is developed into a context that he feels he must paint. Sometimes he never returns to it. It is remarkable, however, when looking through the hundreds of sketches that he has kept over the past forty years, how small a proportion have not, in one form or another, found a place in a finished composition; a result not of an arrogant belief that every idea he has is important, but of the consistency with which his mind shapes his interests.

Colville's procedure for making a painting is scrupulously thorough, literally bringing "the shadow of an object" into substantive form. He works through a series of drawings, beginning with imaginative sketches and then developing a carefully measured geometric modular structure. As a final step he makes life drawings, which he proportions to the chosen module. He paints on pulped wood boards prepared with an acrylic base and gesso sanded smooth. The modular structure for the painting is then transferred onto the board. He paints over it, first with thin washes and then gradually, over a period of perhaps three months, he builds up the forms in finer detail to an even opaque finish. He finally seals the surface with a varnish. Since 1963 he has worked exclusively with acrylic paints, and he ensures the chemical stability of the works by using the same building agent in the gesso, paint layers, and varnish. Prior to 1963 he had worked principally with casein tempera, a technique in which powder colours are saturated in casein, the protein of milk. His use of oil paint was primarily restricted to his student and wartime works, and to the period from 1956 to 1963.[7] The fast-drying properties of both tempera and acrylic best suit his multi-layered technique. The result is a perfectly smooth, sealed surface, complemented by a frame that he designs and builds himself.

The care he takes with the physical make-up of his paintings reflects the precision with which he constructs their images. He works with relatively few elements in any particular painting, each one carefully chosen and sited. It is a classic procedure, in the sense that nothing could be added or taken away without damaging the image as a whole. The motto of the seventeenth-century French painter Nicholas Poussin, an artist whom Colville much admires, applies equally to him: *"Je ne rien néglige"*–"I overlook nothing." This motto can guide us in approaching the paintings, for they are to be looked at with a care equivalent to the process by which they were made.

The best introduction to Colville's work comes by looking closely at one of his most recent pictures, one in which his process and technique is fully developed. I have said that Colville frequently includes himself in his pictures, but it is rare, very rare that he openly faces the spectator. We can only properly describe one painting as a self-portrait, this is *Target Pistol and Man* (CR 117) painted in 1980, the year Colville turned sixty.[8]

The picture makes an immediate and striking impact. Each element is presented with decisive clarity, each form exactly described in shape, texture, and space. Yet the picture, so clearly constructed, so tightly locked, is somehow not at rest. It calls for completion. Is there a key to it, a hidden clue that will set it still? Do we need to find a category for it? A category would at least give us a framework in art to approach it. If, for instance, we could see it in photographic terms, as a painstaking transfer from a photograph, we could recognize it as a frozen moment from a continuous action. If we

fig. 1
Study for Target Pistol and Man
    November 26, 1979
Pencil and ink
30.3 x 22.7 cm
Collection the artist

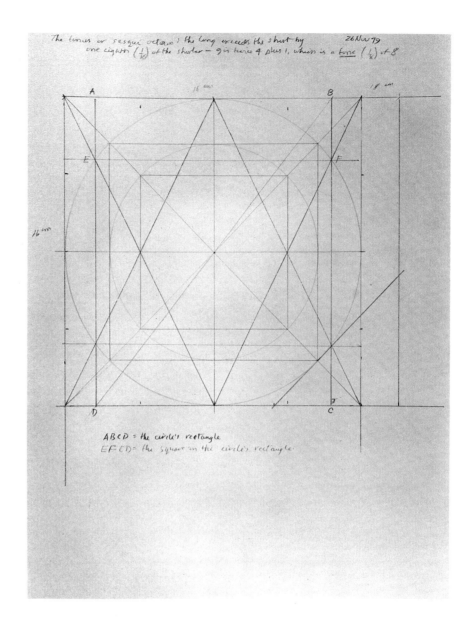

could look at it in terms of narrative then we would find ways to reconstruct its past and project its future. If we accept the picture as a self-portrait, then it could be a painted soliloquy, an image of soul-searching for which the pistol stands both as a symbol for and an instrument of death. Or is it that the picture is simply a way to tug at the spectator's attention, an imposition into his space backed up by the threat of aggression?

The picture appears to be open to all these speculations and yet fully served by none of them. To approach it in these terms would be like reading a paraphrase of a poem instead of the poem itself. To begin by asking what a painting means, rather than to recognize what we see, is to bypass the painting itself and fix its identity, as we would any other object, with a name.

If we can say that the elements in the picture are immediately clear, we are describing the way they are ordered. In effect, we are talking about the construction of space. This painting, like every one that Colville has made since 1950, is based on a precise, mathematical scheme (fig. 1). And even if the exact technical and conceptual details are not immediately recognized, we grasp intuitively a sense of satisfaction from the structure. Some aspects of *Target Pistol and Man*, however, are easily described: the central vertical axis bisects the figure of the man; horizontally the picture is divided into three sections with the window and its frame, the table, and the intervening area of wall and floor each occupying one third of the picture's height. The sense of stability comes from the way that the man is enclosed by a circle inscribed within the square of the picture's format, his heart at the centre of both figures–this circle determines the positioning of his elbows and head and the slope of his arms.

It is difficult to go much further without the aid of a ruler and compasses, and although this would reveal a whole series of correspondences, it would not settle the sense of unease we feel from the picture. For within this structure are vital asymmetries: the man is set with his left elbow closer to us than the right, and the direct gaze of his eyes is offset by confronting us with the pistol on one side and by the windows on the other side. We look past him, as if for an escape route.

The ambiguity between stability and unease is but one layer of contrasting characteristics in this painting, as it is in all his mature pictures. There is also the contrast between the plausibility of the scene (we can believe it to have happened, even if we cannot explain it) and its constructed artifice. They divide our attention between the picture's emotional and psychological effect and the intellectual satisfaction of realizing how finely it has been constructed.

This layer of contrast merges with another, that between the anonymity of the work and its specific character. In its technical structure Colville seems determined to protect the anonymity of the image. The forms are painted with no display of gesture or surface variation; each element is given the same attention and sharpness of focus. The painting even lacks the personal mark of a signature and its title is simply descriptive. The image itself appears unyielding; the face of the man–clinically acute in its description–gives nothing away by its expression, the room in which he is seated is sparsely and impersonally furnished, and his clothing simple and dark.

Nevertheless, we cannot get away from the insistent specificity of the picture. Its anonymity seems in conflict with the sheer clarity of its presentation. How can we reconcile its public with its private address? The lack of personal expressiveness seems to give it a generic quality that should be equally meaningful to any spectator. Yet we know this is not the case, first because it is a specific and unique object and second because we respond to it through our individual senses and experiences. The public face of the image is, ultimately, intensely private. Are we, as spectators, brought to face a person, any person, or are we in a privileged position, observing the artist in self-reflection?

To approach the painting through such layers of contrast focusses on the essential character of Colville's work. Ambiguity is discovered not as a barrier to understanding but rather as its condition, leading us to the centre rather than casting around for "meaning" or turning away in speculation. Our first reaction may be to see the picture in terms of violence, as if the man is contemplating murder or suicide. But we cannot say which, and the very fact of our uncertainty reflects on the nature of painting itself. All paintings rest on illusion and Colville's realism draws the spectator's attention to this fact. In *Target Pistol and Man* it is manifested in the contrast between a direct address to the spectator and a mirror image of the artist. The irony is that the painted image allows the simultaneous existence of both. What is more, the artist does not show himself in the act of painting but in an attitude that can only be real as a direct address to the spectator, or as a totally private reflection. Every way that we approach the picture we are trapped by the web of our own thought.

Colville has always made it clear that his concern as an artist can only be with his experience, that he must say of every situation, "I, and only I, am experiencing this."[9] From this follows his dependence for his subjects on people and situations very close to him. He is, therefore, not only an observer of those people and situations, but the observer also of his reactions to them. Usually when he includes himself in a picture, it is in a subsidiary role; as though his making the picture is a reflection back onto a situation in his past. He shows himself as a part of that experience and as its observer. This is why *Target Pistol and Man* is so unusual. He faces himself openly, but in doing so is trapped between the illusion of his image, the reality of himself, and the activity of his making a painting.

The painting is one of self-reflection emotionally and literally. The image, set in Colville's studio, is mirror-reversed. Allowing for that reversal, the circumstances in the picture are precise. The principal fall of light on the figure comes from above, not from the windows behind him. This means that the position of the mirror into which he was looking when making the picture – and hence the position occupied by the spectator – is on the wall where he has his easel, a wall lit by a skylight.

fig. 2
Self-Portrait 1963
Silverpoint on gessoed masonite
26.7 x 34.9 cm
Dr. Helen J. Dow

Although Colville frequently uses himself as a model, *Target Pistol and Man* is the only painted self-portrait, properly speaking, in his mature work. Its origin, however, can be traced to a group of drawings that he made in May 1963, some seventeen years earlier, in response to a commission he received for a self-portrait. A silver-point drawing (fig. 2), the only one he ever made in this subtle but demanding technique, was the final result.[10] The setting was the attic studio of his home in Sackville, New Brunswick. The series begins reflectively but quickly moves toward an attitude of self-confrontation (fig. 3), in which the searching description of the pen-and-ink drawing is covered with layer on layer of dark wash. The use of the wash layers gives a sense of dynamic transformation, like the ghastly changes that come over the portrait of Dorian Gray in Oscar Wilde's story. Colville himself has said (as have other artists in different words),

> Art is one of the principal means by which a human tries to compensate for, or complement, the relentlessness of death and temporality.[11]

These drawings seem to reflect on that idea, permanently fixing the identity of the artist within a context of inevitable change.

Target Pistol and Man draws certain aspects directly from the 1963 composition – the artist in his studio, the confrontation with the self and the spectator. But the confrontation is more disturbing as our attention constantly wavers from the man to the pistol and beyond to

fig. 3
Study for Self-Portrait May 21, 1963
Ink wash and white paint
27.2 x 35.4 cm
Collection the artist

the window, only to return to the piercing frankness of his eyes. In the course of working on the preparations for the picture, he made important changes. One drawing (fig. 4) shows that he first thought of the picture in a circular format. This gave the composition a compressed form, with the man enclosed in the circle and the gun placed directly in front of him. A few days later he introduced the square format (fig. 5); this sets the man more comfortably in the space – the angles formed by his arms are less sharp and the loose clasp of the hands, slack at the wrists, echo the horizontality of the window ledge and the radiator. And the pistol, instead of lying as a barrier between the man and ourselves, is set to one side. But if this change seems to make the man more relaxed, it heightens the unease for the spectator. In the earlier sketches, with the pistol directly in front of the man, his tense, compressed form made it seem that the weapon belonged wholly to his concerns. With it set to one side, just below his hand, it is an extension of him and directed at us. The aim of the pistol has become our business.

To be able to follow the process of this work through the drawings stretching over so many years gives us a special insight into Colville's creativity. Colville himself tends to think of his drawings in a way that parallels T.S. Eliot's feelings about the various drafts of his poems, that "posterity should be left with the product, and not be encumbered with a record of the process."[12] Although it is, in the end, the finished poem and the completed painting that bears the meaning and must

fig. 4
Study for Target Pistol and Man
    November 28-30, 1979
Pencil and ink
30.3 x 22.7 cm
Collection the artist

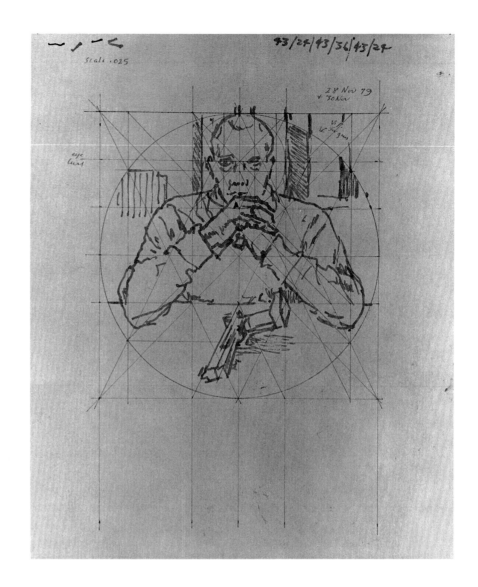

stand the scrutiny of criticism, it is valuable to be able to watch the progress of a work in order to gain a special appreciation of its integrity, its independence, and depth. In the final analysis, however, we must face the literal fact of the painting. The drawings are just one aspect, the painting is the result of the artist in his totality – his thought, his experience and his skill. The painting, to follow John Dewey's notion of conclusion, is not simply the final step, but the containment of the whole process.[13]

In looking at Colville's paintings we have, in the end, just two directions in which to go. If we expect from the work a "solution," then we will try to see it symbolically or as part of a narrative, even as a

fig. 5
Study for Target Pistol and Man
    December 18, 1979
Pencil and inks
30.3 x 22.7 cm
Collection the artist

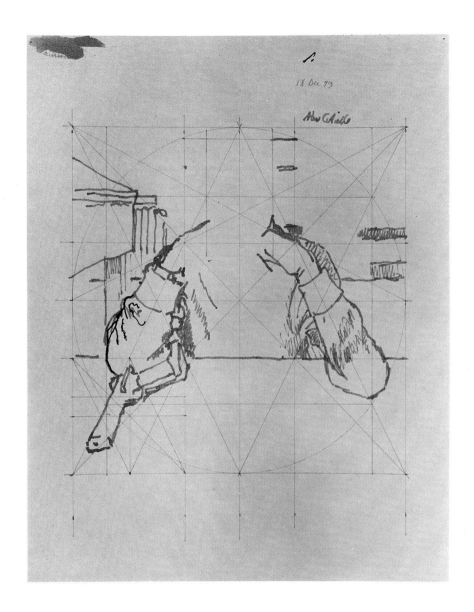

painted photograph. But I believe that we must start with the literalness of the picture and our experience of it. We have its objectivity and our subjectivity, an inversion of the process by which the artist made it. Colville's concentration on a small number of objects in any one painting and the precision with which he relates them to each other focusses our attention; the picture's ambiguities lie not in what we see but in how our seeing leads us to think.

Let us focus in *Target Pistol and Man* on just one aspect, the most compelling and disturbing relationship in the picture, that between the man and the pistol. The pistol is specific in its type and unambiguously identified in the title of the picture; it is a target pistol. (In one preparatory drawing he showed the pistol lying on a target.) It is not, therefore, an instrument designed to kill or injure, but to test the focus and aim of the man who holds it. It extends his range, linking what he sees along its sights with a mark on the target that records the accuracy of his concentration and coordination. Seen that way, the pistol can be any pistol and the man, any man. But we know that what we are looking at is a painting, an object brought into being by the specific intention and action of one man. That object is the result of the specialized extension of the artist to the picture's surface, the result of the focus and the aim of his attention, brought about through the instrument of his brush. It is thus self-reflective, recording both the artist's view of himself through the metaphor of the target-shooter, and the reality of his activity in making the painting. The artist as man, the man as artist is the final ambiguity, real and inescapable.

Alex Colville at age eleven near Tidnish,
Nova Scotia, where the family had a summer
cottage.

Colville at age 17 in 1938, with his parents
outside their home in Amherst, Nova Scotia.

Alex and Rhoda Colville on their wedding
day in 1942 in front of Rhoda's parents' home
in Wolfville, where the Colvilles themselves
have resided since 1973.

Top: Canadian war artist Colville, stationed
in London, England, in 1944; bottom left:
Colville in 1957 with Sam, who later became
the subject of *Hound in Field* and was felled
by a train at age fifteen months; bottom
right: Rhoda Colville in 1942 in Pembroke,
Ontario, near Petawawa, where her husband
was stationed in the army.

A Colville family portrait taken in 1951; from
left to right: John, Graham, Alex, Rhoda,
Ann, and Charles.

Governor General Jules Léger presents a
copy of the Governor General's medal
designed by the artist to Alex Colville at
Rideau Hall in 1976. The Colvilles were
frequent guests at Rideau Hall during the
time the medal was being designed.

Colville's dealer Wolfgang Fischer took this
portrait of the artist in 1980 at Evangeline
Beach near Wolfville, where the Colvilles
have a cottage.

Colville on the balcony of his apartment in
Berlin in 1971, overlooking the River Spree.

TWO

THE EARLY YEARS: THE ARTIST AT THE THRESHOLD

The order and clarity in Colville's work reflects the decisions he has made about his life and career. If he did not know the precise direction his art would take, he was certain from the start about the way in which he would have to work. He has, for example, deliberately stayed apart from the centre of artistic events, although not from a lack of concern with the progress of the visual arts in Canada; he has willingly participated over the years in numerous committees and juries. His detachment has been for two reasons. First, once he had found his artistic direction his need to concentrate completely on it outweighed the value he felt was to be gained by constant contact with other art. The second reason has been his attachment to the Maritimes, particularly the Annapolis Valley region of northwestern Nova Scotia, and to the family life he has developed there. This bond is rooted in his background and in that of his wife Rhoda, who was born in the house in Wolfville built by her father and in which, since 1973, the Colvilles have made their home.

Colville's work is founded on a powerful affinity to a sense of place both geographically and emotionally. He describes himself as a deeply conservative person, which expresses a commitment to values of life and thought more closely tied to a rural than an urban environment. It is from this position that he declares his beliefs and relationships, not through sealed images and inaccessible symbols, but through reflecting the openness and directness of the person that he is. His need for communication is not that of a diarist, who *tells*, but that of an individual who shares.

David Alexander (Alex) Colville was born in Toronto on August 24, 1920. His father, David Harrower Colville, had immigrated to Canada in 1910, at the age of twenty, from Markinch, a small coal-mining town in Fifeshire, Scotland. He married Florence Gault of Trenton, Ontario, in 1914 and the couple settled in Toronto around 1920 after living in Moncton, Cape Breton, and Trenton. Colville Senior was employed in steelwork construction; his wife had worked as a milliner before her marriage. Their first child, Robert, was born in 1915. In 1927 the family moved to St. Catharines on the Niagara Peninsula and, two years later, when Alex Colville was nine, to Amherst, Nova Scotia. Colville Senior became a plant supervisor at the Robb Engineering Works there, having worked for its division, the Dominion Bridge Company, in Ontario.

Colville's mother, a practical and clear-minded woman, opened her own business in Amherst. She was, Colville recalls, a person who knew the value of everything; in contrast to his father, who despite the rigorous and often dangerous work he did, was a romantic and ultimately an unfulfilled man. The family was Roman Catholic but, although he made no open declaration, Colville early on denied for himself the value of organized religion. When he went into the army he marked down his religious denomination as "United Church" because that seemed to indicate fewer expectations for open religious performance.

In 1929, shortly after moving to Amherst, Alex Colville caught pneumonia from which he almost died. His recovery was long and slow. The experience, in retrospect, had a profound effect on him:

> All through that spring and summer I led an almost solitary life.... I became what we usually call an introvert, one whose life is essentially a kind of inner life. I began to read, really for the first time, and I did quite a few drawings...cars, boats, airplanes.[1]

The doctor who attended him, Dr. Goodwin, a man of broad interests, became something of a mentor to him; "I am sure that knowing him was one of the things that made the idea of becoming an artist legitimate to me." When Colville was fourteen he enrolled in a weekly art class offered by Mrs. Sarah Hart from nearby Sackville. He attended her classes for three years and through them came to meet Stanley Royle (1888-1961) from Mount Allison University. Mrs. Hart invited Royle each year to comment on her pupils' efforts; Colville's work attracted Royle, who encouraged him to continue his art studies at university. Colville had already decided to go to Dalhousie University in Halifax to study law and politics, and he had been awarded a scholarship. To change courses would have meant a heavy financial burden on his parents, but Royle persisted and arranged for an equivalent scholarship to be offered Colville to study art at Mount Allison. He enrolled there in September 1938. Of his family's reaction he has said,

> My parents approved; they would not have done so had they been more acquainted with the middle-class mores of that time.[2]

Mount Allison University in Sackville, with a School of Fine and Applied Arts housed in the Owens Art Gallery, was one of the few universities in Canada to offer fine arts and the first to grant a Bachelor's degree in the subject. When Colville enrolled there, Stanley Royle was the Director of the museum and school, a position he had held since 1935 when he left the Nova Scotia School of Art in Halifax. A Yorkshireman who had trained at the Sheffield School of Art, Royle held the position at Mount Allison for ten years, retiring in 1945 and returning to England.

The formation of Colville's visual vocabulary came first from the European paintings at the Owens Art Gallery. In addition to his regular teaching, Royle organized a summer school each year. Colville attended this in each of his student years, going to Prospect, Nova

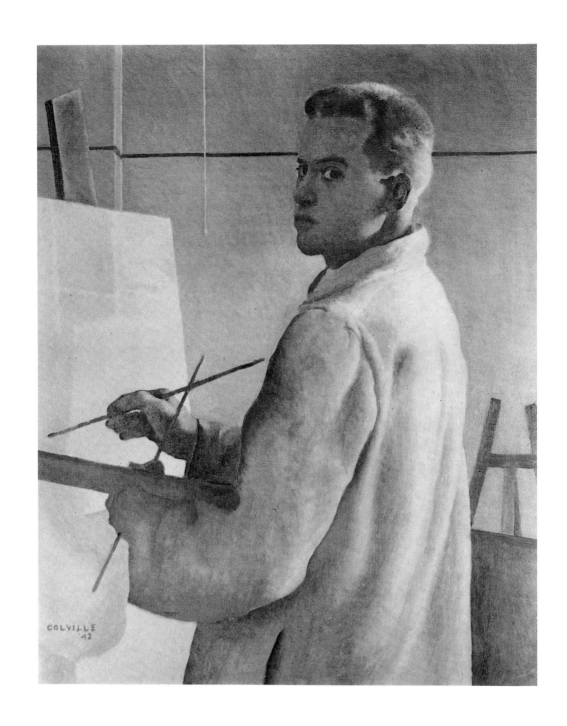

Self-Portrait 1942
Oil on canvas
Dimensions unknown
Destroyed
Catalogue Raisonné No. 154

Scotia, in 1939; Peggy's Cove in 1940; and Woodstock, New Brunswick, in 1941. A small number of paintings made during these summer sessions appear to be the only ones to have survived from his student period. A few other examples, subsequently destroyed, are known through photographs (CR 152-154). A small oil on canvas-board painted at Prospect in 1939 is probably his earliest extant work (CR 149). It shows the influence of Royle's Post-Impressionist style but has a firmness of design and an assured handling of paint. With Royle's encouragement Colville submitted work for exhibition and was included in the Art Association of Montreal Exhibition in 1941 and at the Royal Canadian Academy of Art in 1941 and 1942.

Colville graduated from Mount Allison University in the spring of 1942 and immediately enlisted in the 1st Canadian Army, with the ambition of becoming a war artist. While still a student he had been asked to do a poster for the Wartime Information Bureau and had met Colonel A.F. Duguid, Head of the Army's Historical Section in Ottawa. Duguid suggested to Colville that he join the army as a war artist, although the Official War Artists' program was not approved until January 1943.[3] The first step was to get a commission and Colville went to Brockville, Ontario, for officer training. Things, however, did not go smoothly for him and he was soon "returned to unit," probably, as he thought later, for being "too independent-minded."[4]

Assuming this ended his war-art ambitions he settled down to other duties, first in Fredericton and then at Camp Petawawa in the Ottawa Valley. He worked his way through the ranks to sergeant and was recommended for a commission, which he received in September 1943. All this time, Colonel Duguid had been following his progress, apparently against the advice of the civilian war art advisory panel, consisting of H.O. McCurry, Charles Comfort, and A.Y. Jackson.[5]

On the basis of the financial security that the army offered, Colville married Rhoda Wright, who had also been in the Fine Arts program at Mount Allison, in August 1942. But his relatively settled existence was changed with dramatic suddenness. In May 1944 he was sent to England. Upon arrival at Canadian Military Headquarters in London he was told he had been appointed an official war artist. Over the next two years he made a large group of works, of which one hundred and twenty-six are preserved in the Canadian War Museum Art Collection.[6]

Colville had not done any painting in the previous two years and was given two weeks with a Royal Army Service Corps unit in Yorkshire to orient himself to his work. He was then seconded to the Navy and sailed to the Mediterranean to record the troop landings in the south of France. He made a substantial group of drawings and watercolours in the six weeks he was there, and then returned to

England to make paintings based on his field work. At the end of October he joined the 3rd Canadian Infantry Division and remained with that unit until September 1945, following the fighting through Holland and into Germany.[7]

With no opportunity to establish a professional career for himself, Colville's war art was a direct extension of his student work. Left very much to himself he quickly developed full-time work habits:

> Everyday I would go out with this jeep and driver. Anything that I saw that was kind of interesting, I would make a drawing or watercolour of it. So it was a kind of genre painting of everyday life in the army....The parallel I would make would be for a novelist to be a police reporter doing factual reporting, physical, sordid, concrete, rather than philosophical or abstract.[8]

But it had to be more than strict reportage for that was best served by movies and photographs. "You are not a camera," Colville has said, "you are doing essentially different things. There is a certain subjectivity, an interpretive function."[9]

There is a gradual shift in the priorities of his interpretations. In the major pieces done in the Mediterranean there is an emphasis on action, such as *The Deploy,* where his view is as a participant reacting to the impression of the moment. Later in Europe his work stresses the prelude to action, its aftermath and the long periods of inactivity. His work often showed considerable poignancy, for instance, the watercolour *Grave of a Canadian Trooper* where the destruction of a man and a machine, lit by the brilliance of spring sunshine, are set in parallel.

His single most affecting experience was being sent to the Belsen death camp a few days after it had been liberated. He made a watercolour and some drawings there and later used these as the basis for an oil painting (CR 11). He has said of this experience:

> This being at Belsen was strange...the thing one felt was one felt badly that one didn't feel worse.... There is a certain point at which you begin to feel nothing.... It was a profoundly affecting experience. Obviously it would be, unless a person was a complete fool. You were bound to think about this quite a bit.[10]

It was as if the sheer enormity of the horror was too much to absorb and too much to express. Even as it demanded the utmost of his efforts and attention it would never be possible to transmit the feelings with any adequacy.

In practical terms his experience as a war artist was great training and discipline but, equally important, it pointed up the difference between recording and creating. The war work *presented* subjects to him immediately; his later work was the result of a long and slow inventive process. The direction in which he wanted to go appears in two of the wartime oil paintings, *Tragic Landscape* and *Infantry Near Nijmegen, Holland* of 1945 and 1946 respectively (CR 10 and 14). *Tragic Landscape* seeks to make a single death into a broad statement on the futility of war. The signpost serves both as a grave marker and a symbol of military territorial objectives; the cow represents the continuity of life. The picture has all the seriousness and difficulty of early attempts at universal themes. *Infantry Near Nijmegen, Holland* is more successful in marking the transition from the immediacy of an event into a considered statement. Colville wrote in his diary, "On February 1, I envisaged my first big canvas – the subject being infantry marching in single file along a road."[11] The painting is effective because of its simplification and concentration of mood; as close as the soldiers come to us they remain, with their downcast eyes, indifferent to our presence.

After the close of hostilities in May 1945 Colville helped organize a War Art exhibition in Amsterdam and visited Paris, spending two important days in the Louvre. In October 1945 he was reunited with his wife Rhoda and saw, for the first time, his son Graham who had been born in July 1944. The couple subsequently had three more children, John born in 1946, Charles in 1948, and Ann the following year. He finished out his service career in Ottawa making oil paintings based on sketches he had done in Europe.

Colville then had to face the question of a post-service career. The choice appeared to be teaching or commercial art. At that moment he was offered a teaching post at Mount Allison University, in the art department from which he had graduated just four years before, and which was now under the chairmanship of Lawren P. Harris, son of the Group of Seven painter. Colville accepted the offer without hesitation and moved with his family to Sackville. He remained there until settling in Wolfville in 1973, although he had resigned from the university in 1963 to devote himself full-time to painting.

The decision to give up teaching was a difficult one. He had enjoyed and benefited from discussions with students and his fellow academics on a wide range of topics. Most immediate, however, was the matter of financial security. Even though his work was selling well, the prices he was getting were small in relation to the needs of his family. The pace of his work was slow and his production did not markedly change after 1963. But it was a step he felt was essential, and toward the end of the 1960s events began to move firmly to his advantage.

In the 1950s and early 1960s Colville had sold work through a number of commercial galleries, including the Hewitt Gallery in New

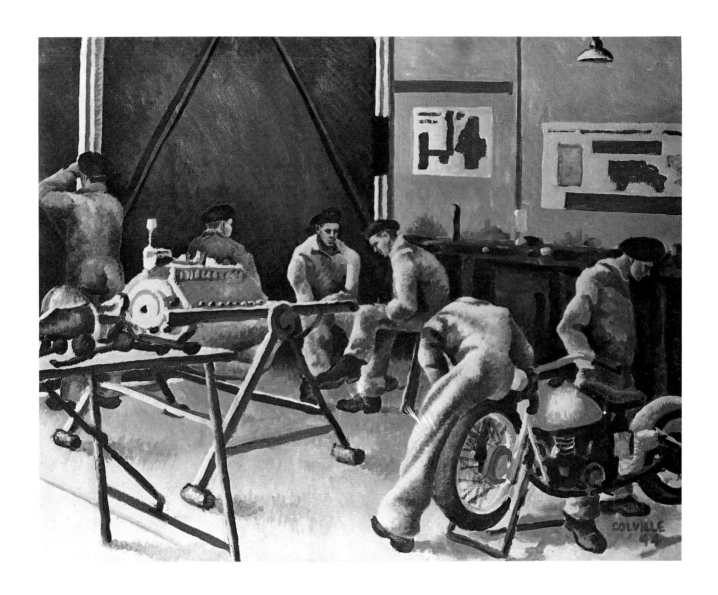

Fitters "Break" Period 1944
Oil on canvas
61.0 x 76.2 cm
Canadian War Museum/National Museum of
  Man/National Museums of Canada
Catalogue Raisonné No. 1

Mechanical Transport Park 1944
Oil on canvas
58.4 x 73.6 cm
Canadian War Museum/National Museum of
  Man/National Museums of Canada
Catalogue Raisonné No. 2

Tank Transporter Tractors No. 2 1944
Oil on canvas
76.0 x 60.7 cm
Canadian War Museum/National Museum of
    Man/National Museums of Canada
Catalogue Raisonné No. 6

45

Nissen Huts at Night 1944
Oil on canvas
40.6 x 50.3 cm
Canadian War Museum/National Museum of
    Man/National Museums of Canada
Catalogue Raisonné No. 5

Convoy in Yorkshire No. 2 1944
Oil on canvas
76.3 x 102.0 cm
Canadian War Museum/National Museum of
    Man/National Museums of Canada
Catalogue Raisonné No. 3

Nijmegen Salient 1944
Oil on canvas
76.4 x 102.0 cm
Canadian War Museum/National Museum of
  Man/National Museums of Canada
Catalogue Raisonné No. 9

HMCS Prince Henry in Corsica 1944
Oil on canvas
76.2 x 101.6 cm
Canadian War Museum/National Museum of
   Man/National Museums of Canada
Catalogue Raisonné No. 7

Messerschmitt 1946
Oil on canvas
60.7 x 81.2 cm
Canadian War Museum/National Museum of
     Man/National Museums of Canada
Catalogue Raisonné No. 12

LCA's off Southern France 1944
Oil on canvas
101.4 x 76.0 cm
Canadian War Museum/National Museum of
 Man/National Museums of Canada
Catalogue Raisonné No. 8

Exhausted Prisoners 1946
Oil on canvas
76.2 x 101.6 cm
Canadian War Museum/National Museum of
  Man/National Museums of Canada
Catalogue Raisonné No. 13

The Nijmegen Bridge, Holland 1946
Oil on canvas
91.5 x 122.6 cm
Canadian War Museum/National Museum of
   Man/National Museums of Canada
Catalogue Raisonné No. 15

Bodies in a Grave, Belsen 1945
Oil on canvas
76.2 x 101.3 cm
Canadian War Museum/National Museum of
  Man/National Museums of Canada
Catalogue Raisonné No. 11

York, Dominion Galleries and Watson Gallery in Montreal, Banfer Gallery in New York, and Laing Galleries in Toronto. This changed in 1966 with his inclusion in the Venice Biennale. Dr. Harry Fischer, then associated with Marlborough Fine Art in London, saw his work and immediately offered exclusive support. Colville's relationship with the Fischers has continued ever since, through Harry Fischer's establishment of Fischer Fine Art in London in 1972 and since 1977 with Dr. Wolfgang Fischer, who took over the business after his father's death. From 1978 he has also been represented in Canada by the Mira Godard Gallery in Toronto.

Over the years Colville has been approached on a number of occasions for commissions; he did two major works for Mount Allison University when he was on staff there (CR 20 and 64). In the past twenty years, however, he has been very selective about commissions. Of the few he has accepted the most notable are the designs for the Centennial coins done in 1965 and minted in 1967 (CR 146) and the commemorative medal for the Governor General and Mrs. Léger in 1975 (CR 148). The years have also brought with them recognition in the form of honours and responsibilities through serving on committees. He was made an Officer of the Order of Canada in 1967 and raised to Companion of the Order in 1982. He holds honorary degrees from seven Canadian universities and in 1981 was appointed Chancellor of Acadia University. He has, on two occasions, spent extended periods away from home, both times as Visiting Artist. He was at the University of California at Santa Cruz for the academic year 1967-68 and in 1971 spent six months in Berlin under the *Berliner Kunstlerprogramm*. His responsibilities have included membership on the Visiting Committee of the National Gallery of Canada and board membership of the National Museums of Canada.

He has valued over the years friendships with people from various walks of life, among others, George Grant, the philosopher; Lincoln Kirstein, the ballet impresario; Charles Forsyth, a United Church minister; and Harry Fischer. Although he has been acquainted with many artists he has not developed close relationships with any of them; he has simply not been drawn to seek out such contacts. He rarely visits contemporary art exhibitions, although when travelling he will invariably spend time in the Old Masters galleries.

Modern literature and thought, however, are a different matter. The experience of reading Sartre and Camus in the 1940s and 1950s was of profound importance to him. "It seemed," he has said, "enormously significant in a way I don't think anyone could comprehend today."[12] He learned a great deal in regard to visual thinking from reading André Malraux and Bernhard Berenson. From fiction he has been particularly drawn to Joseph Conrad, John dos

Passos, Ford Madox Ford and, in more recent years, to Saul Bellow and John Updike, the latter both as novelist and critic. But his reading and interests are far-ranging, including poetry, science, psychology, as well as philosophy and fiction.

The war left Colville with a whole series of unanswered questions, both personal and professional. Not the least of these was: how could he meaningfully develop his art? He spoke about this period of his career in a talk given at the New Brunswick Museum in 1951 on the occasion of his first solo exhibition, organized by Avery Shaw. He said, "When [the war] was over, I was rather bewildered in two ways."[13] The first was his need to come to terms with the great art of the past. The highlight of his visit to Paris in 1945 had been the two days spent at the Louvre, where he had been particularly impressed by Manet's *Olympia* and Egyptian art.

His second cause of bewilderment was more difficult to express. He spoke of

> the lack in me of [a] total concept of war, or perhaps I should say a clear attitude towards the war.… Men of my generation lacked the impetus which produced so much good art in the early twenties – [namely] disillusionment with war. We could neither be disillusioned (partly because we had few illusions to begin with) nor could we be starry-eyed about the war.[14]

At first glance these two concerns seem a curious combination. But they point directly to Colville's search for lasting and substantial values, both in his life and in his art. His visits to the Louvre and other European galleries brought him for the first time to the substance of art history and how he stood heir to it. He saw it not as a sequence of images, names, and dates, but as a manifestation of the realities that men have understood. The impact of Egyptian art brought this home to him most strongly; he recognized in its hieratic and stable forms, the physical presence of transcendent values. It set a mark for him that in his own art he has never doubted.

This sense of art history was his recognition of one great event; his "bewilderment" over the events of the war was another. What did it mean to have been witness to the greatest episode of human destruction? He had been an observer of events of which he was a part; how was he to reconcile his subjectivity with a perspective on the larger scale of events? These issues he had to settle as he faced the question of what to paint. Slowly he came to realize that his way was not through abstract themes but through an acute and considered observation of his immediate circumstances and surroundings.

Centennial Year Coin Designs 1965
Various sizes
Catalogue Raisonné No. 146

Fox and Hedgehog 1972
Open gold medallion on chain, edition 12
4.7 cm width
Catalogue Raisonné No. 147

Governor General's Medal 1975
top: gold; centre: plaster; bottom: drawing
Gold coin: 5.2 cm diameter
Catalogue Raisonné No. 148

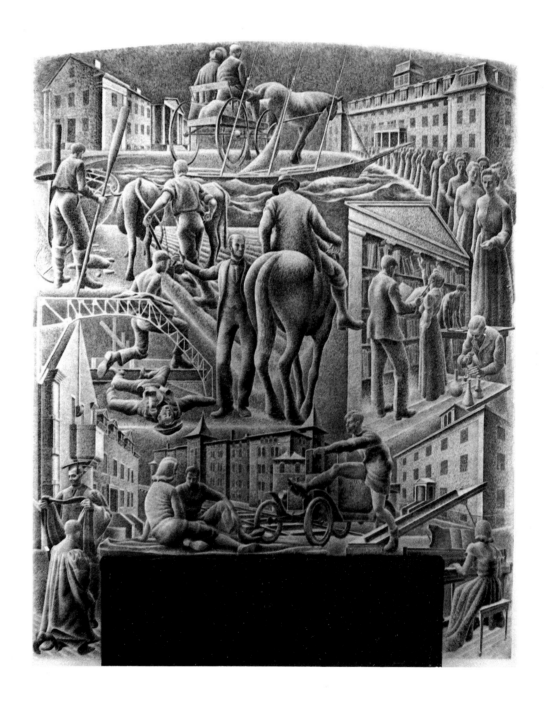

The History of Mount Allison 1948
Egg tempera on gessoed wall
4.9 x 4.1 m
Collection Owens Art Gallery, Mount Allison
   University, Sackville, NB
Catalogue Raisonné No. 20

Colville's move to Sackville in 1946 was, in the result, the right one for the serious development of his work. His teaching job meant security and the opportunity to paint, and the university's isolation from major centres of artistic activity gave him the freedom to set his own pace. At that moment it was essential to be distanced from the further stimulation of other art; "I realized," he said, "that it might take me years, for instance, to absorb the effects of the two days that I spent in the Louvre."[15] Progress was slow and difficult. He made just six paintings in his first four years there and felt fully satisfied with none of them.

His largest work was *The History of Mount Allison* (CR 20), a mural commissioned by the university. Comprising a potpourri of scenes in the manner developed by the Mexicans Diego Rivera and José Orozco, it was his only painting of the immediate post-war years to include the human figure.[16] It was a type of work historical and social in subject, still being heralded in Canada during the 1940s as having potential for the future, although it failed to sustain much further interest.[17]

Of the five other paintings produced between 1946 and 1949, three are landscapes and two are animal pictures. The latter, *Three Horses* of 1946 and *Group of Horses* of the following year (CR 16 and 17) are reminiscent of Georges Seurat's early paintings, at least in mood and brush-handling, if not in brilliance of colour. Seurat was an artist whom Colville regarded highly, sharing his interest in ancient Egyptian art and admiring his ability to invest contemporary subjects with a sense of stable and serious presence. The horse was the subject of two of Colville's most dynamic paintings of the 1950s, *Horse and Train* and *Church and Horse* (CR 43 and 71), but in the earlier pictures he seems to have chosen it for its placid strength. The animals are "at peace" and indifferent to human concerns, much as the cow in *Tragic Landscape* (CR 10). His interest in painting horses was also an expression of his own background; his grandfather in Scotland had been a carter and had traded in pit ponies, and his father had a life-long interest in horses.

The landscapes of these first four years at Sackville, *Windmill and Farm*, *Railroad over Marsh*, and *Racetrack, Sackville* (CR 18, 19, and 21), are symbols of human events and relationships. In *Windmill and Farm* the economic and social conditions that allow the construction of the farm are, as it were, made possible by the harnessing of nature through the windmill and the harrow. In *Railroad over Marsh* we see the imposition of man into the landscape by his means of communication, the railway tracks, and telephone wires. Communication, whether interpersonal or implied through mechanical devices, was to become a major theme in Colville's later works.

Group of Horses 1947
Oil on canvas
71.1 x 96.5 cm
Whereabouts unknown
Catalogue Raisonné No. 17

Railroad over Marsh 1947
Oil on canvas
60.9 x 81.3 cm
Beaverbrook Art Gallery, Fredericton
Catalogue Raisonné No. 19

Racetrack, Sackville 1950
Oil on gessoed panel
60.9 x 98.5 cm
Art Bank of Nova Scotia
Catalogue Raisonné No. 21

fig. 6
Two Figures, n.d.
Brush and ink
35.1 x 27.1 cm
Collection the artist

More important than these paintings were his figure drawings of the same period. These led to his paintings of the early 1950s, which set the direction of his mature work. Almost exclusively concerned with the female nude in a seashore or architectural setting, each element – figure, sea, architecture – carried with it a long, essentially immeasurable history of artistic representation. He wanted to use subject matter that was deeply rooted within the human psyche. He spoke of this in his 1951 talk:

> What I have in mind is the use of material so old, so often used down through the ages, that it has become an integral part of human consciousness,…'an infinite reverberation of the past.'[18]

By giving this reverberation visible form, drawing it out of the subconscious, the artist transcended the personal to touch the "collective self-awareness." He had to make concrete the fundamental questions – "Who are we? What are we like? What do we do?"

Colville's view of the artist's purpose, carrying social as well as personal responsibilities, bears closely on Jung's description of the artist's process. In his 1922 lecture *The Spirit in Man, Art, and Literature* Jung had said,

> The creative process, so far as we are able to follow it at all, consists in the unconscious activation of an archetypal image, and in elaborating and shaping this image in the finished work. By giving it shape, the artist translates it into the language of the present, and so makes it possible for us to find our way back to the deepest springs of life. Therein lies the social significance of art: it is constantly at work educating the spirit of the age.[19]

His search for subject matter brought Colville to the work of Henry Moore. Moore, through his study of the figure sculpture of early societies, had developed a dynamic approach to sculpture, one that related the human figure, the landscape, and the natural materials of the sculpture, whether wood or stone.[20] Colville first learned of Moore's work during the war – Moore's *Shelter Drawings* had brought him national attention for the first time – but it was only in the late 1940s, through the encouragement of the New Brunswick painter Miller Brittain, that he began a close study of the sculptor's work.[21] Several of his paintings of the early 1950s have a distinctly Moore-like character in their approach to figures, solid in mass and devoid of detail (CR 24 and 26).

A composition for which Colville made several drawings between 1948 and 1950 (fig. 6) is even more important in showing his approach to "timeless" subject matter. Two figures, standing on either side of a frame structure, mediate between the sea and the man-made

Nudes on Shore 1950
Glazed tempera
60.9 x 98.5 cm
Beaverbrook Art Gallery, Fredericton
Catalogue Raisonné No. 24

Tragic Landscape 1945
Oil on linen
60.9 x 91.6 cm
Canadian War Museum/National Museum of
    Man/National Museums of Canada
Catalogue Raisonné No. 10

Infantry Near Nijmegen, Holland 1946
Oil on linen
101.6 x 122.0 cm
Canadian War Museum/National Museum of
    Man/National Museums of Canada
Catalogue Raisonné No. 14

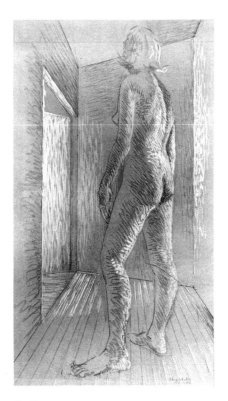

fig. 7
Nude in Corridor January 17, 1949
Pencil, ink and white paint
47.6 x 27.0 cm
Collection the artist

fig. 8
Nude in Doorway February 2, 1950
Pen and brush in ink
37.6 x 28.0 cm
Collection the artist

structure. This structure represents human limitations, for it quickly loses all sense of scale and proportion as it pushes out into the sea. The composition (Jungian in its sense) reflects on humankind as conscious and rational to a certain point, unconscious and irrational to an unknowable degree.

The most crucial picture of the immediate post-war period was one which broke with the predominant seashore scenes. Colville has often said this painting, *Nude and Dummy* (CR 22) of 1950, was the first that he felt had been in major part successful. Although related to the early compositions with figures and architecture, it introduces two new elements; a more specific setting and a sharply focussed relationship between the two figures. Its origin is to be found in sketches Colville made several years earlier. The first, from February 1949 (fig. 7), shows a nude woman standing in a corridor, hesitating and yet attracted toward a brightly lit doorway. A year later, again using a domestic interior, he made a drawing (fig. 8) where the figure hovering on the threshold is held between the curious sequence of spaces behind her and the attention of the spectator. Colville, in giving shape to his ideas, places himself at the crossing point between the observer and the observed. It is the position expressed by the contemporary French poet Edmond Jabès when he wrote, "My place is at the threshold" ("*Ma place est au seuil*").[22] Self-awareness may allow him to project himself by imagination beyond the threshold, but not to pass through it. It is a thought sharpened by Jabès word-play between "*seuil*" and "*seul*"; between "threshold" and "alone."

Colville in his paintings stands at the threshold between the private world and the public. He gives of himself to the individual spectator by his viewpoint, opening a way for the spectator. The figure in the drawings seems to be a creature of Janus, the double-faced Roman god of doorways and thresholds and the ruling divinity of beginnings. We could think of Janus as Colville's household god, for the notion of a double-facing and double-faced figure appears so often in his work. It is at the core of some of his most important statements.

With these sketches Colville was not moving toward a specific subject. They are no more than the shadow of an image, a fascination that will somehow bring a female figure in a deserted interior together with the observing artist. They seek to draw something to the surface, to substantiate it before it recedes, like trying to capture a dream image which is so clear until the moment of description.

Then, quite suddenly, the direction of the image was resolved. He made a sketch on March 1, 1950, (fig. 9) setting two figures in an empty room, by the shape and slope of its ceiling, probably an attic. Our viewpoint is from the door of the room, on the threshold of the space, looking at one figure walking in front of the windows and having the

fig. 9
Study for Nude and Dummy March 1, 1950
Pencil and ink
12.0 x 13.4 cm
Collection the artist

second standing so close to us that she is cut off by the frame. From here Colville worked quickly through a series of sketches, establishing the relationship between the two figures as they circulate in the room, defining its space. Then his thinking changed. The nearmost figure, already truncated top and bottom, is further reduced by the elimination of her left arm (fig. 10); and then just prior to starting the painting he transformed the figure into a dressmaker's dummy (fig. 11).

Nude and Dummy was the first painting in which Colville used a unified perspectival scheme. It was an important change in procedure for him, taking him away from Impressionist composition "by eye" to a rational formation of pictorial space. It was, in retrospect, a logical step, arising out of his concern with the reality of the painting itself, that is, with what a painting could "say." It was logical also in that he never doubted that the business of painting lay in the direct transposition of images from the three-dimensional world into the two-dimensional terms of painting. Painting for him was a matter of construction; its process should be clear and precise.

The basis of a unified pictorial perspective had been developed in Florence early in the fifteenth century. Painters quickly adapted the principles of the system to be able to bring an appearance of "life-likeness" to their pictures. It became a device, almost a trick. But

Three Horses 1946
Oil on canvas
50.8 x 66.0 cm
Collection Art Gallery of Ontario, Purchase,
  1946
Catalogue Raisonné No. 16

Nude and Dummy 1950
Glazed gum arabic emulsion
60.9 x 81.2 cm
New Brunswick Museum, Saint John
Catalogue Raisonné No. 22

Coastal Figure 1951
Glazed tempera
60.9 x 139.7 cm
The Artist
Catalogue Raisonné No. 28

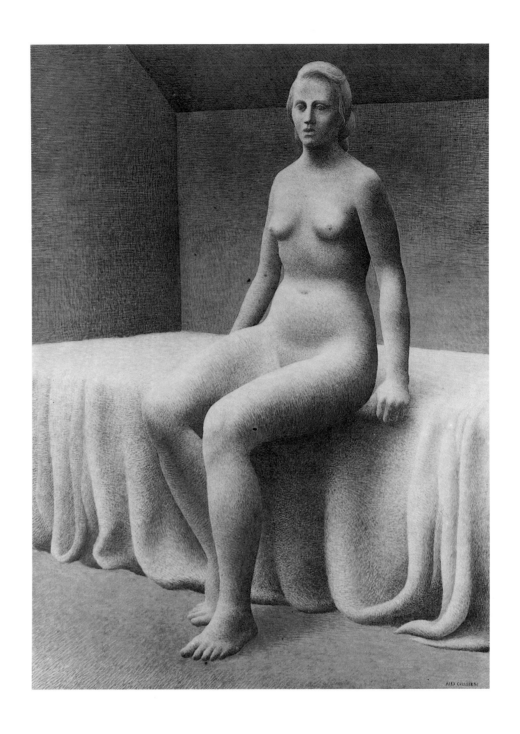

Seated Nude 1951
Glazed tempera
81.2 x 86.3 cm
The Artist
Catalogue Raisonné No. 25

Four Figures on a Wharf 1952
Casein tempera
35.5 x 71.1 cm
National Gallery of Canada, Ottawa
Catalogue Raisonné No. 30

Three Girls on a Wharf 1953
Glazed tempera
41.3 x 25.4 cm
Collection Mr. & Mrs. Christopher Ondaatje
Catalogue Raisonné No. 38

fig. 10
Study for Nude and Dummy March 14, 1950
Pencil
15.2 x 20.2 cm
Collection the artist

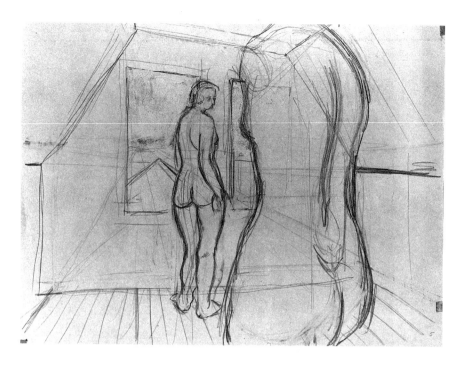

behind that device lay the desire to express a rational relationship between the appearance of the world and a belief in its essential order, a universal order based on mathematics. As has often been pointed out, the system does not in fact describe the way we see, but over the years the convention of linear perspective has set the standard in the Western world by which images are judged in relation to "reality." It has become a part of our language, even though its original philosophic and religious bases have long been abandoned. And despite the fact that modern painting has altered, criticized, and dismissed even their pictorial premises, the conventions of linear perspective continue to persist in our acceptance of images and illusions of space.

Colville's development of pictorial space in *Nude and Dummy* and in the paintings that followed is substantially based on the device of linear perspective. In this sense his work remains in contact with the conventions of spatial description that have dominated pictorial depiction for four hundred years. It is not that Colville subscribes to a universal mathematics; but this system, and others he has subsequently developed, was a means to give rational and concrete form to the contents of his imagination and experience. He does not paint "slices" from the real world but makes constructions from the complex processes of his perceptions, his experience, and his memory. His pictures are symbols of this process, not simply a record of the natural world nor the contents of a dream world.

Although we can trace the origin of *Nude and Dummy* through the

fig. 11
Study for Nude and Dummy 1950
Inks and watercolour on grey paper
30.5 x 40.6 cm
Collection the artist

drawings, its catalyst arose from a different set of circumstances. Colville, dissatisfied with the progress of his work, decided in the summer of 1949 not to paint when his teaching year finished but to spend the time renovating his Sackville home. With his customary thoroughness he made detailed, measured plans and then with the help of a student, proceeded with the work. He has said:

> I realized years later that this was an absolutely crucial experience for me.... The business of working on an actual building and making an environment was the thing that enabled me to get this idea of figures in a specific environment rather than just a kind of vague nothingness as in the previous compositions.[23]

The work of construction and the creation of an environment for living was transferred to his painting.

Nude and Dummy reflects measurement, a point made explicit when he replaced one of the figures with the dressmaker's dummy. The purpose of a dummy is wholly contained in the notion of measurement and the painting presents an interlocking scale of measurement; first that between the woman and the domestic architecture, second, between the woman and the dummy. The picture is concerned with standards; it responds to the way we orient ourselves to the world through the structures and conventions of measurement we use. Painting too, in its ordering of illusions, has its conventions of measurement.

Woman, Man and Boat 1952
Glazed tempera
31.7 x 48.9 cm
National Gallery of Canada, Ottawa
Catalogue Raisonné No. 34

Girl on Piebald Horse 1952
Glazed tempera
57.7 x 35.5 cm
Collection Dr. & Mrs. Daniel Silver
Catalogue Raisonné No. 33

fig. 12
Two Seated Figures March 21, 1952
Ink
38.0 x 38.1 cm
Collection the artist

The breakthrough that *Nude and Dummy* signified for Colville was not, however, immediately followed. Several paintings of the early 1950s refer back to the wartime period, especially subjects of departure and of the celebration of return. One of them, *Soldier and Girl at Station* of 1953 (CR 36), is specific in terms of locale; but others, like *Four Figures on a Wharf* and *Woman, Man and Boat* both of 1952 (CR 30 and 34), are abstract in event and setting. *Four Figures on a Wharf* is an abstraction of memory, a reflection on Colville's desire to return home and be reunited with his wife. But by giving it a loosely classical ambience he suggests his concern is with the essence, not the actual fact, of "waiting." We cannot identify specific fears and longings in the women; they are anonymous, even in the characterless drapery that they wear. We are turned back from them to the painting's viewpoint, as if we are standing on the shore, literally and figuratively standing back from events, creating an idealized image of memory.

A similar notion is described in *Woman, Man and Boat* begun at the end of 1952; the return from overseas and the moment of greeting are stated in reduced and abstracted terms. All movement whether in the girl, the sea, or the boat is eliminated. The activity of the painting

Soldier and Girl at Station 1953
Glazed tempera
40.6 x 60.9 cm
Private Collection
Catalogue Raisonné No. 36

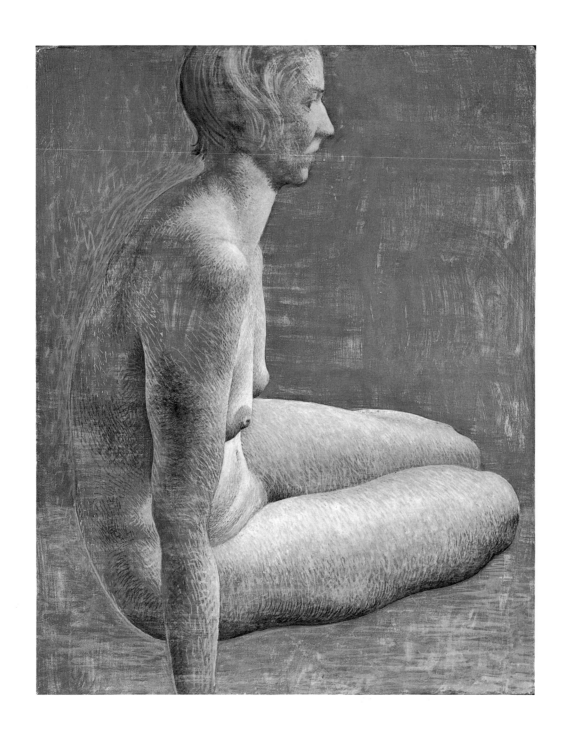

Seated Nude 1950
Glazed tempera on masonite
50.8 x 40.6 cm
Dr. Helen J. Dow
Catalogue Raisonné No. 23

Woman on Wharf 1954
Casein tempera
24.1 x 15.2 cm
Dr. Helen J. Dow
Catalogue Raisonné No. 42

comes from its structure, establishing the line of contact between the eyes of the man and the woman. The elimination of detail, the locking of one form with another, and the solid formation of each element, even of the sea, stills the event to an abstraction, not a narrative, of feeling.

This reduction of incident and detail to heighten contact between the observer and the observed is further intensified in *Woman, Jockey and Horse* (CR 31) also of 1952. It derives from earlier seashore drawings (fig. 12), and in the echoing between the figures anticipates pictures of the later 1950s. The curve of the woman's dress and the neckline of the jockey's shirt, the intricate pattern of her hair and his striped cap link the figures visually. But drawing them together serves only to distinguish them; the jockey seems stiff, the woman relaxed; he is merged with the horse, she stands free from it. Her independence and control over the situation is heightened, paradoxically, because her face is concealed; we can only respond to her through the jockey. He appears dependent on her, his eyes open to her image, his ear ready for her word. It is a dependence symbolized by his jockey's colours; his status restricts his personality to the specialized fact of his occupation. This sense of dependence is a vein that runs deeply through the whole of Colville's work. It is a reflection on himself as an observer, as someone who fully realizes himself only through validating his experience by a specialized occupation, that of painting. He casts himself in the role of observer, whether from outside the picture or, as in *Woman, Jockey and Horse,* by using his own features for the man, from inside the picture. So often, he makes himself an object of his own observation and dependent on the figure of a woman.

Woman, Jockey and Horse 1952
Glazed tempera
38.1 x 50.8 cm
Private Collection
Catalogue Raisonné No. 31

Two Boys Playing 1952
Glazed tempera
50.8 x 50.8 cm
Collection Mr. & Mrs. William Teron
Catalogue Raisonné No. 32

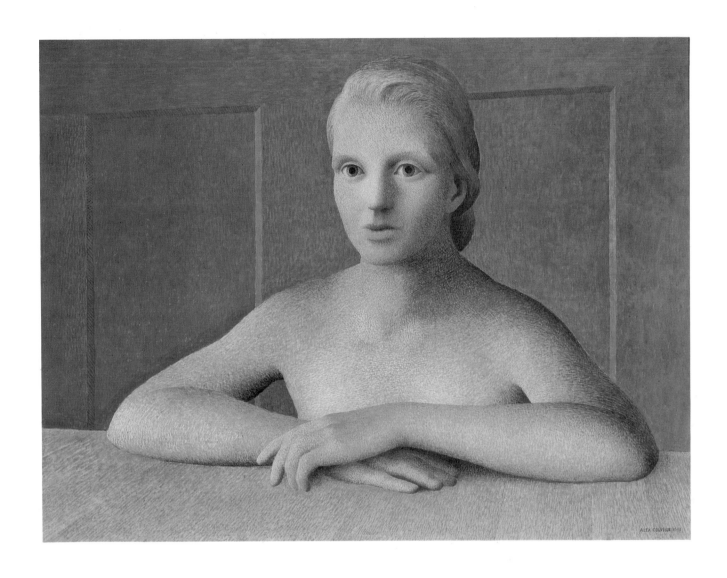

Woman at Table 1951
Glazed tempera on board
60.9 x 81.2 cm
Private Collection, Ottawa
Catalogue Raisonné No. 27

Racer 1954
Casein tempera
45.7 cm diameter
Private Collection
Catalogue Raisonné No. 39

THREE

THE MID-FIFTIES: ART AS AUTHENTICATION

Colville's work of the mid- and later 1950s was marked by major change and substantial achievement. Outside the wartime works, it remains his most prolific period. Between 1953 and 1958 he made twenty-five paintings, nearly a fifth of his present *oeuvre*, and in 1955 pulled his first serigraph edition, a technique that he has continued to use regularly.[1] These years also marked the spread of recognition for his work. In 1958 he wrote to Donald Buchanan, then editor of *Canadian Art*:

> I am now in a position which I would never have believed likely – the demand for my work exceeds the supply. It is perhaps a passing phenomenon and does not cause me to be puffed up.[2]

Twenty-five years later, the phenomenon still shows no signs of passing.

In 1952 he made his first visit to New York. He took some photographs of his paintings with him and showed them to Edwin Hewitt, who ran a gallery specializing in American artists loosely defined as "Magic Realists." Hewitt immediately accepted his work, including him in a group show in 1952 and giving him a one-man exhibition in 1953. A further group show in 1954 was followed by a second solo exhibition in 1955, the year that Hewitt closed his gallery. During that first trip, Hewitt introduced Colville to ballet impresario Lincoln Kirstein. Kirstein bought a number of Colville's paintings during the 1950s and was instrumental in bringing the artist's work to the attention of collectors in the United States.

During the same period Colville made important sales of work to public collections in Canada; the National Gallery of Canada acquired *Child and Dog* and *Woman, Man and Boat* in 1954, *Four Figures on a Wharf* in 1955, *Family and Rainstorm* and *Woman at Clothesline* in 1957 (CR 29, 34, 30, 49, and 53). In 1959 they bought *Couple on Beach* and *Hound in Field* (CR 55 and 56). The Art Gallery of Toronto (now the Art Gallery of Ontario), which had been the first public gallery to acquire one of his pictures, *Three Horses*, in 1946 (CR 16), added *Elm Tree at Horton Landing* (CR 52) to its collection in 1956. In these years also Colville's work was included frequently in exhibitions of Canadian art both here and abroad, establishing his reputation as one of Canada's leading contemporary artists. It was the period, in short, in which he developed a distinctive style through a series of compelling and curious images.

The paintings from the mid-1950s, more directly than in the earlier work, show Colville's concern with communication. Although expressions of what was personal and individual to him, they carry the capacity to interest and move others. Colville has described how making a picture is

Children in Tree 1957
Casein tempera
47.6 x 54.6 cm
C-I-L Inc.
Catalogue Raisonné No. 54

Family and Rainstorm 1955
Glazed tempera
53.3 x 71.1 cm
National Gallery of Canada, Ottawa
Catalogue Raisonné No. 49

the working out, or the clarification and concretizing of some sort of trauma, which is my trauma, [and which] works, at least in some instances, for the person who looks at the painting.[3]

The essential aspect of this exchange is that of viewpoint; how his experience is given into the experience of others. Viewpoint combines two levels of meaning; it is from his viewpoint that the choice of subjects is determined and it is through the structure of the pictures around their viewing point that the image is conveyed. In his earlier paintings, as we have seen, Colville had avoided too close a personal identification with the subject matter by using timeless symbols and a cool painting style. He opened a gap between the subjective and the objective through the distancing effect of metaphor, and through a sculpturesque simplicity that echoed the past rather than substantiated the present. By these means he had tried to avoid jeopardizing the communicability of his images when expressing the private nature of his experience. This effort was most difficult when it touched on the strongest of his feelings, in pictures such as *Four Figures on a Wharf* and *Woman, Man and Boat* (CR 30 and 34), having to do with the wartime separation from his wife and the longing for return. And yet, precisely because of that difficulty, they were valuable and telling subjects.

The success he felt was achieved in *Nude and Dummy* (CR 22) had come from the clarity and rigorousness of its construction. Some ten years earlier the American poet Wallace Stevens had written of the expression of feeling and imagination in relation to poetry and painting. His remarks relate closely to Colville's situation. Stevens wrote:

> If one says that a fortunate poem or a fortunate painting is a synthesis of exceptional concentration…we find that the operative force within us does not, in fact, seem to be the sensibility, that is to say, the feelings. It seems to be a constructive faculty, that derives its energy more from the imagination than from the sensibility.[4]

In those pictures of the early 1950s that were not concerned with memories of separation and the longing for return, Colville's viewpoint and the spectator's engagement with the image were more directly stated. He used a variety of dynamic means: asymmetry, imbalance, and surprise. In *Child and Dog* (CR 29), for example, he identifies with the viewpoint of the child so that, without distortion or threat, the dog towers over the little girl. The compressed space of the image, focussing attention on the relationship between the child and dog, responds to the direct and immediate concerns a young child has with her surroundings. But even though the subject matter comes

Child and Dog 1952
Glazed tempera
81.2 x 60.9 cm
National Gallery of Canada, Ottawa
Catalogue Raisonné No. 29

Woman at Clothesline 1956-7
Glazed oil emulsion
121.9 x 91.4 cm
National Gallery of Canada, Ottawa
Catalogue Raisonné No. 53

Visitors are Invited to Register 1954
Casein tempera
35.5 x 48.2 cm
Mendel Art Gallery Collection, Gift of the
    Canadian National Exhibition
    Association
Catalogue Raisonné No. 44

directly from the artist's experience – the child is his daughter, the dog was the family pet – the sculpturesque style, reminiscent of the early fifteenth-century Florentine Masaccio, and the low viewpoint bring the spectator firmly and swiftly into the picture's world.

Sometimes the viewpoint is literally and metaphorically eccentric, for instance in the 1951 painting *Two Pacers* (CR 26). Helen Dow, in her discussion of the picture, noting that the elimination of details thrust the emphasis onto the dynamics of the image, found that "speed became the virtual subject."[5] But how is that sense of speed achieved? Certainly not through the style and drawing of the animals, for even if they are anatomically correct they appear to be cast in stone. As the Impressionists in the later part of the nineteenth century discovered from studying photographs, a painter's ability to depict movement and energy in a swift-moving animal was not guaranteed simply by extracting one frame from a sequence of "real" images. A spectator, particularly if he does not have a specialized knowledge of pacing horses, reconstructs an image that brings a complex series of actions into a unified dynamic image in space. But this is not what Colville has painted.

The picture presents an eccentric combination of two viewpoints. The first viewpoint is ours as spectators of the picture, the second that of the man who is watching the event. The geometry of the picture sets the eye-level of the man at the same level as the viewer's. The vanishing point of that structure lies at the fence on the extreme left, so that sight-lines from the heads and hoofs of the horses lead to that point through the head and feet of the man. The man's position gives him a natural view of the event; our immediate view, from in front of the horses, is possible but unusual. Together the two viewpoints form an inversion between reality and imagination; we are presented with both a normal view of the event "from the sidelines," and a privileged, imaginative one. The low viewpoint and Colville's elimination of essential details, such as the axles of the wheels, harness for the horse, and a seat for the driver, thrusts the emphasis of the picture onto the spectator. We can look to the man for a sense of objective security, but we cannot escape the plunging horses suspended over us.

This picture and *Horse and Train* (CR 43), which followed two years later, bring Colville close to Surrealism. The images jolt us by their unexpected juxtapositions and angles and they contain the apprehension of disaster found, for instance, in the paintings of the Belgian artists René Magritte and Paul Delvaux (fig. 13). They followed André Breton, who had argued that the capacities of the unconscious mind, made apparent in dreams, were a reality more marvellous and more true than the filtered and censored forms of the conscious mind. This could be shown by setting disparate objects

fig. 13
Paul Delvaux (Belgian, 1897-)
Sleeping Venus 1944
Oil on canvas
172.7 x 199.2 cm
The Tate Gallery, London

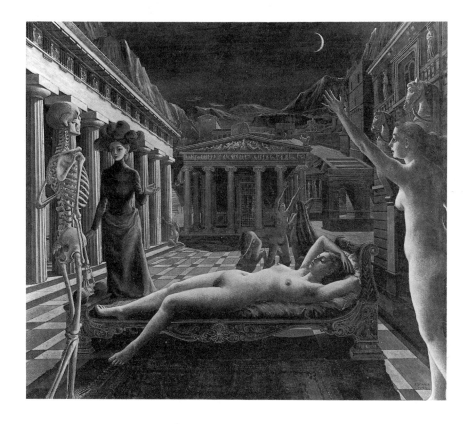

together and drawing from their synthesis a new reality; if they do not normally stand together they can be *thought* together.

The idea for *Horse and Train* first appeared on a sheet of sketches dated March 16, 1954. Colville made horizontal and vertical versions of the composition, both with the same elements. He also wrote on the sheet, "a dark horse against an armoured train." This refers to the poem "Dedication to Mary Campbell" by the South African writer, Roy Campbell. It was one of two introductory verses to a collection of his work published in 1949.[6] Campbell had gained some notice in North America through his publications and through two lecture and reading tours he made in Canada and the United States. The first tour was made in 1953 and included a stop at Mount Allison University in Sackville. Colville, then on the university staff, met him and was encouraged to read his poetry.

The two lines from the poem to which *Horse and Train* refers are:

Against a regiment I oppose a brain
And a dark horse against an armoured train.

In her analysis of the picture, Helen Dow read these lines as a reference to Colville's wartime experience. Finding that the horse "quite evidently symbolizes the artist," she describes the painting in

Two Pacers 1951
Glazed tempera
60.9 x 81.2 cm
Private Collection, Ottawa
Catalogue Raisonné No. 26

Horse and Train 1954
Glazed tempera
40.0 x 53.3 cm
Art Gallery of Hamilton, Gift of Dominion
　Foundries and Steel Limited, 1957
Catalogue Raisonné No. 43

terms of an opposition between animal and machine; "this horse represents all that is human pitted against all that is inhuman, feeling against mechanism, mind against matter."[7] But this, I think, is not the point either of the picture or the poem that inspired it. The context of Campbell's poem was his concern about the assertion of the individual against mass behaviour. The lines form, in their meaning, an inverted couplet; the regiment and the armoured train stand for all that is conventional in thought and behaviour, the minds of people capable only of pushing along on fixed rules. The brain and the dark horse represent the opposition of the individual against mass behaviour. A dark horse is, of course, an idiom for an unconventional and secretly thinking individualist. And Campbell explicitly identified himself this way when, in 1951, he published his autobiography under the title of *Light on a Dark Horse*.[8]

In the poem the opposition between the dark horse and the armoured train forms an immediate and powerful image, linked directly to the opposition between the regiment and the brain. Colville, in making the painting, could not shade the description of things into abstract qualities; his images had to be direct, explicit, and concrete. But he also had to avoid a sense of narrative, and he removed the image from the natural flow of time to prevent common sense from projecting the confrontation of horse and train to a disastrous conclusion. The painting, like the poem, has its own reality to which each aspect and each tone is special. Its meaning is suspended in the precision of its presentation and the associations it opens in the spectator's mind.

We cannot say simply that the horse *is* the artist or that the train *is* the machine. We can take Campbell's view that a dark horse symbolizes the individualist. But we can also say that it is a *dark* horse in the sense that whatever the horse may see is "dark" to us. Although animals inhabit our world they remain essentially unknown to us and indifferent to our concerns. The horse is undisturbed by the oncoming train because of that indifference. One way of thinking of a dark horse, however, does not preclude others; on the contrary, one way can suggest others as long we are not concerned about the painting having a "solution," a fixed and definitive reading. And all readings (viewings) are poetically sharpened by the natural shock and surprise of the image. Our conventions of normality are challenged. We are provoked by the fascination of facing the unknown, brought to the edge of something that no amount of rationalizing will resolve.

Colville's art is suspended in the gap between imagination and reality. The surprise to the imagination must be set against visual images whose elements are so strikingly convincing that we are forced to deal with them as if they are real. To achieve this synthesis the

Illustration for "The Ball Poem" by John Berryman 1956
Casein tempera
22.8 x 15.2 cm
Private Collection, Montreal
Catalogue Raisonné No. 51

Couple on Beach 1957
Casein tempera
68.5 x 91.4 cm
National Gallery of Canada, Ottawa
Catalogue Raisonné No. 55

Elm Tree at Horton Landing 1956
Oil emulsion
121.9 x 91.4 cm
Collection Art Gallery of Ontario, Gift from
    the McLean Foundation, 1958
Catalogue Raisonné No. 52

Ballad of the Fox Hunter 1959
Serigraph, edition 25
45.7 x 25.4 cm each; 4 panels
Catalogue Raisonné No. 127

process of what Colville calls "authenticating" is crucial. He has described the beginning of all his images as a "kind of fantasy" in which, more often than not, the notion of a particular setting determines how the fantasy will be realized. It then becomes a matter of bringing that fantasy to an authentic image so that the work has

> the kind of immediacy that films have [and] this means what I think of as authenticating the thing so that it is not just a kind of an abstract or symbolic [train], but a very specific, actual thing.[9]

In the case of *Horse and Train* the setting of the picture is at Aulac, just outside of Sackville, where the elevated track crosses the Tantramar Marshes. One night Colville stood beside the track as a train approached, to fix in his eye the glistening of the headlight on the rails and the complex tonal structure of the scene. This authenticating procedure was further developed through the 1950s as he moved away from the generalized settings of the early works. It remains a vital element in the construction of his works.

Horse and Train is one of the few pictures to which a precise text can be related. Two other works of the 1950s, *Illustration for "The Ball Poem" by John Berryman* (CR 51), a commissioned work of 1956, and *Ballad of the Fox Hunter* (CR 127) of 1959, a series of four serigraphs based on W.B. Yeats' poem, also have direct literary sources. But in those two cases his intention was specifically to illustrate the poems. *Horse and Train* is its own poem and this approach, along with the development of the process of authentication, set the standard for the major works of the mid- and later 1950s.

One of his most ambitious works of this period was *Family and Rainstorm* of 1955 (CR 49). The work is ambitious in the complexity of its textures, in its combination of landscape, human figures, and the automobile, and in the subtlety of its tonal values, unified to silver greys. It is ambitious also in the way that it casts a mood in a specific time and place. The pose of the woman relates directly to a 1950 drawing (fig. 6) that he used two years later in *Woman, Man and Boat*. There she was an allegorical figure of greeting; in *Family and Rainstorm* she is specific. The family is based on Colville's own, his wife Rhoda, and his youngest and eldest children, Ann and Graham. The location, too, is specific; on the shore of the Minas Basin looking northward to the Blomidon Peninsula. The viewpoint of the picture is high, placing the spectator (and the artist) two or three steps behind the woman and completing the steep diagonal of the figures leading into the car.

Colville has spoken of the picture in terms of "acceptance." A family day at the beach has been curtailed by the threat of rain. But the figures accept the disappointment without complaint. It is an attitude

Nude on Rug 1954
Casein tempera
38.1 x 30.4 cm
Private Collection, Ottawa
Catalogue Raisonné No. 41

Prize Bull 1954
Casein tempera
30.4 x 38.1 cm
Manuge Gallery, Halifax
Catalogue Raisonné No. 40

that is philosophically conservative, with something about it of Epicurus' *ataraxia*, which describes the qualities of tranquility, equanimity, and repose in the face of life's circumstances so as to overcome superficial and irritable responses to what is unchangeable.[10] The family represents, in an ideal sense, a stability in harmony with nature, here expressed by the fact that the figures do not stand out against what cannot be avoided. It is expressed also in the unified tones and textures, in the subtle interactions of colour, and in the way the shapes of the figures echo the landscape. Acceptance in this sense means harmony, not defeat, reflecting responsibility onto the spectator, who is drawn in as though he is the picture's fourth figure, stepping into the place of the artist.

Two years later, in *Couple on Beach* (CR 55), Colville divides the act of observation by moving the watching figure forward so that he participates in the picture, while still facing the direction we, as spectators, take. The woman lies relaxed and closed onto herself. The forms and colours of the sand, sea, and sky, echoing one another, support and reflect the form of the woman. But the man is hunched and awkward, physically present but psychologically distant from the scene that he observes. We see not only what he sees but also his vulnerable and self-conscious attitude. How different this is in self-attitude and confrontation with the spectator from a painting like *Self-Portrait with Patricia* of 1936 by Stanley Spencer (1891-1959), an artist for whom Colville has much regard. The overt sexuality, compressed viewpoint, and unidealized figures in Spencer's painting seem to challenge the spectator, forcing him into the discomfort of unintentional voyeurism. In Colville's painting the discomfort is that of the man within the picture, both observed and observing the harmony between the woman and her surroundings.

Colville's picture raises an acute awareness of the nature of relationships, of closeness and separateness, of overcoming the void of absolute aloneness through accepting the responsibility for realizing oneself as a separate individual. In particular this means the awareness of being separate from those people to whom one is closest and on whom one's dependence is greatest. Colville has said, "I am inclined to think that people can only be close when there is some kind of separateness."[11] When he says this he does not mean the egotism of "having one's own space," but rather the responsibility of caring for the individuality of the other. Seen this way, Colville's view of himself, as it is reflected in *Couple on Beach*, is not one of pessimistic alienation, but of an awareness of what it means to observe. The fact that the woman's head is concealed makes the nature of the event precise: "What is being contemplated is the woman, the sea, the sky."[12] But only through our eyes, not his.

Dog and Horse 1953
Glazed tempera
38.1 x 50.8 cm
Mr. & Mrs. J.L. Black, Sackville, NB
Catalogue Raisonné No. 35

Child with Accordion 1954
Casein tempera
38.1 x 38.1 cm
Private Collection
Catalogue Raisonné No. 47

Colville's emphasis on specific places, setting his images in familiar contexts, was a way to give form to the notion of life's continuity; to be drawn to a place or a setting is a way of showing the continuity of the individual with history. One picture where this is given, for him, an unusual form is the 1956 painting *Elm Tree at Horton Landing* (CR 52); unusual because it contains neither people nor animals. The tree marks a place of considerable importance in the history of the Grand Pré region; there is a local belief that the Acadians were expelled from this point. The setting is an isolated spot on the Gaspereau River as it leads into the Minas Basin. The elm is the only tree of substantial size in the immediate area and its age is legendary. The tree's roots have been revealed by erosion of the river bank and despite suffering lightning strikes it still flourishes. The painting thus marks a special value of time and place, in the landscape and history it reflects. It continues, at another level, the sense of continuity and stability represented by the *Family and Rainstorm*.

Paintings like *Family and Rainstorm* and *Couple on Beach* are the work of a fully mature artist. The realization of Colville's meaning is made possible by a total confidence of style; he does not suggest, he *shows*. It is from this vantage point, recognizing the depth of Colville's mature work, that it is valuable to consider the context from which Colville's art developed, especially its relationship to the painting of artists who, in the very broadest sense, belong to the American Realist movement.

The first attempt to identify and categorize contemporary American Realist artists was in 1943, when the Museum of Modern Art's *American Realists and Magic Realists* exhibition showed contemporary artists alongside nineteenth-century painters like George Caleb Bingham, Thomas Cole, and Thomas Eakins, and two living artists of an older generation, Edward Hopper and Charles Sheeler, described as "20th Century pioneers." The exhibition defined two directions: "sharp focus and precise representation," meaning observation of the outer world; and "Magic Realism" for painting "contrived by the imagination." Alfred H. Barr Jr. had defined magic realism in 1942 as

> a term sometimes applied to the work of painters who by means of an exact realistic technique try to make plausible and convincing their improbable, dreamlike or fantastic visions.[13]

The term "Magic Realism" was first developed in the 1920s to describe the post-World War I German painting of *Neue Sachlichkeit*, or "The New Objectivity," a critical reaction to the chaos and upheaval of post-war Germany. Many artists associated with the movement suffered Nazi repression and some, like George Grosz and Max Beckmann, found refuge in the United States. Their work had a significant effect on the socially responsive American artists of the 1930s.

The catalogue of the Museum of Modern Art's Realism exhibition included an introduction by Lincoln Kirstein, and his support for this form of art continued through his association with Edwin Hewitt. In 1950 Kirstein wrote an essay for an exhibition at the Hewitt Gallery called *Symbolic Realists*. In the essay he paralleled their work with that of the Abstract Expressionists by saying that they "take painting for an intellectual more than a manual profession."[14] The Hewitt exhibition included Andrew Wyeth, Paul Cadmus, Jared French, and George Tooker. Two years later Colville joined the Hewitt Gallery.

It is with this group of painters, among contemporary artists, that Colville has most in common. Not that his work belongs to a common style, for what characterizes their work and his is its independence. Rather, this is the context to which his work belongs, and not the regionalist one within which his work has so often been viewed in Canada. Colville's admiration for Canadian painters like LeMoine FitzGerald, Goodridge Roberts, Miller Brittain, and Jean-Paul Lemieux has been one of respect for their individual work, not from any sense of common interests. Colville had been drawn since his student days to the American Regionalist and Social Realist painting of the 1930s and 1940s, particularly that done under the Works Progress Administration programs, established in 1935 to aid artists during the Depression.[15] He admired artists such as Grant Wood, John Stuart Curry, Alexander Brooks, Edward Hopper and, in particular, Ben Shahn.

Among the painters of his own generation, and those associated with the Hewitt Gallery, the two artists with whom it is interesting to compare Colville's work in the 1950s are George Tooker and Jared French. Colville and French are both interested in Egyptian and archaic Greek sculpture and in the Italian Renaissance artist Piero della Francesca. There is further common ground between them in the search for subject matter that carries "an infinite reverberation of the past" that I have described in Colville's earliest post-war work (French was strongly affected by the writings of Jung); but from the mid-1950s Colville's direction became increasingly specific in its attachment to the facts of the external world.

George Tooker is best known for his pictures that stress the alienation of the individual by the faceless fears of urban life and bureaucratic depersonalization. Some of his pictures like *Subway* of 1950 (fig. 14) seem close to Colville's paintings of the late 1940s and early 1950s,[16] but the pessimism of Tooker's work sets in relief the

fig. 14
George Tooker (American, 1920-)
Subway 1950
Egg tempera on composition board
45.7 x 91.4 cm
Collection Whitney Museum of American
    Art, Juliana Force Purchase

essential optimism in Colville's painting. They represent two very
different interpretations of the word "acceptance" – Colville establishes harmony with the reality of existence, and Tooker expresses
alienation. Tooker's work, like that of many American Realists,
expresses a certain rootlessness. This perhaps occurs in Colville's
early works, with their scant and generalized settings for uncom-
municative figures. But whereas Tooker continued to project this
mood of isolation, Colville by the mid-1950s was moving to
substantiate, not to empty, his world. His emphasis on authentication
is not simply a matter of representational accuracy, more importantly
it is an assertion, in positive terms, of the fundamental reality of the
external world. Through his emphasis on his own family and on
settings familiar to him he insists that *here* is reality; one cannot be an
outsider. And his love of animals is matched by his easy acceptance of
the mechanized modern world. Both artists, at different ends of the
scale, assert values about the reality in which we live.

Skater 1964
Acrylic polymer emulsion
113.0 x 69.8 cm
The Museum of Modern Art, New York, Gift
  of R.H. Donnelley Erdman (by exchange),
  1965
Catalogue Raisonné No. 72

FOUR

FALLING INTO WATER: FOCUSSING ON BALANCE AND CONTROL

The American Realist movement was the primary contemporary context from which Colville's work developed, but equally important was his admiration for the painting of the past. His style, particularly in his earlier work, and his interest in perspectival schemes was indebted to Italian Renaissance painting. In it he respected the relationship between rational structural presentation and profoundly felt content. His rejection of organized religious belief systems has not been taken to avoid the profound issues they approach but to face them on his own terms, through his own experience. The art of earlier times showed him how past generations had united serious content with clarity of presentation. The work that has most impressed him offers few surprises: the mosaics of Sant' Apollinare in Classe and San Vitale in Ravenna; the painting of Giotto, Masaccio, and Piero della Francesca; and the mysterious creation of space in the work of Uccello. Colville has no interest in the more anecdotal aspects of fifteenth-century art, and his rejection of most sixteenth-century work is countered by a real appreciation of some seventeenth-century painters, in particular Nicolas Poussin and Jan Vermeer.

Colville has been drawn toward artists who have developed a precise balance between figures and space, a balance in which the monumentality of the figures arises from the clear pictorial structure in which they are set. This is painting in which, as Colville has said, the "subject matter…has deep reverberations with absolutely right formal organization."[1] He is referring to the classical balance of Poussin and the dream-like ambience of Uccello, the quiet interiors of Vermeer, and the profoundly still figures of Piero della Francesca. There is nothing in these artists of the gossip of anecdote, vapid sentimentality, neurotic tension, or ebullient raucousness. Their meaning comes through slow, even cool contemplation of a precise moment of time in space. These moments are absolutely real, whether they be Piero's Christ stepping from (stepping beyond) the tomb or Vermeer's pearlweigher, whose occupation parallels the weighing of souls in the depiction of the Last Judgement on the wall behind her (fig. 15).

"Space," Colville has remarked, "is a substitute for time, so that the only way in the visual arts that you can [deal with] time is [through] space";[2] our recognition of an absolute (in so far as we can understand any absolute) lies in the coincidence of time in space. Through it the mystery of existence is revealed as the reality of existence.

The combination of the monumentality of figures and the crucial coincidence of time and space is perhaps nowhere more vital in Colville's work than in the three-part painting *Athletes* of 1960-1 (CR 64) commissioned by Mount Allison University for its new athletics centre. The opportunity this work gave him was to gather together a number of issues raised in earlier paintings. It was an important

fig. 15
Jan Vermeer (Dutch, 1632-75)
Woman Holding a Balance c. 1664
Oil on canvas
42.5 x 38.0 cm
Widener Collection, National Gallery of Art,
  Washington

challenge in terms of the size of the work and the specific demands of the subject matter, to say nothing of its prominent position in the main hall of the centre.

Colville chose to show the way athletes compete with themselves concentrating on the athletes' use of their bodies. The only reference to team sports (in which he has no personal interest) is in the goalposts in the right panel. But he makes a place for the spectator by including the stands in the middle panel. Being empty, they are like an open invitation to us, related to our viewpoint. The setting is simple in the extreme and our attention is focussed on the disposition of the figures in space; the swimmer tensed to dive, the javelin thrower and the high jumper caught fractionally before the most extended points of their activity, and the runner about to break the tape. Because the swimmer has yet to begin, the essential space lies before her; the runner's space has been conquered and it diminishes rapidly behind him in steep perspective. The high jumper is suspended in his conquest of space so that the distance between the ground and the bar is shown in its totality.

Colville's use of a three-part format was in part dictated by a practical need to ensure that the surface would remain perfectly flat. But the triptych form, where the outer panels are narrower than the centre, tends to suggest a reference to the Renaissance tradition of altarpiece painting. We should not assume a specifically religious content in Colville's painting, but the formal parallel is valuable in thinking about the image. The picture is not an illustration, in the way that his *History of Mount Allison University* showed the life and history of the university. Rather it depicts athletic endeavour as a specialized matrix of time and space, a concentrated way of seeing the dimensions within which all the events of our lives are situated.

We recognize athletic success as a special combination of physical and psychic energy; physical limitations are apparently capable of being extended through mental determination. *Athletes* is an example of the potential of the wholeness of mind and body equivalent to the "example" of spiritual and physical unity that faces the spectator-worshipper in a devotional picture. But whereas in the latter the artist constructs a mythic present, a transcendence of the here and now, Colville's image is concerned with showing how the here and now can be stretched to its utmost limits. He suggests the extent of our reality in time and space by pressing the boundaries of human achievement.

The figure in motion was the subject of several paintings in the years just prior to *Athletes*, for instance *Child Skipping* and *Swimming Race*, both of 1958 (CR 57 and 58), and *Circus Woman* of 1959-60 (CR 61). *Child Skipping*, based on an incident when Colville saw a girl skipping near the Sackville Central School, has like *Athletes* a setting whose spareness contrasts with the girl's self-absorption. She appears suspended between the buildings, the school to one side and a house on the other. The house – we see only its protective roof which implies an inner warmth – contrasts with the angular, efficient, and new structure of the school, standing on land carved out of an open field.

The young girl, suspended between the two buildings but momentarily indifferent to both, is caught between the dominant aspects of her life, home and school. She is of that in-between age when the centre of a child's life is divided between home and parents on one side, school and interaction with peers on the other. It is also a time when the child begins to recognize her own independence, as she realizes that she is part of many different worlds. Within these she must learn of her own individuality, how to be her own person and still balance the demands and expectations that others place on her.

Circus Woman 1959-60
Oil and synthetic resin
66.0 x 76.2 cm
Dr. Helen J. Dow
Catalogue Raisonné No. 61

Child Skipping 1958
Oil and synthetic resin
60.9 x 45.7 cm
Private Collection, Toronto
Catalogue Raisonné No. 57

Athletes 1960-61
Oil and synthetic resin
1.52 x 2.42 m (triptych)
Collection Owens Art Gallery, Mount
    Allison University, Sackville, NB
Catalogue Raisonné No. 64

In picture after picture Colville brings disparate elements into balance, reflecting the complex of demands we face daily. We must reconcile our inner selves with the circumstances of the outer world. The girl in *Child Skipping* does not yet fully see this, absorbed as she is in her game; we, as spectators, can live her future through our pasts. We can reconcile these elements for her, just as we can come to terms with events in our own lives by bringing their movements into a balance that we control. The realist painter must show these abstractions of balance and control by physical means. This is nowhere more apparent in Colville's work than in his 1964 picture *Skater* (CR 72).

Skater was for Colville a particularly challenging picture to make. The exact shaping of the silhouette was crucial to convey the dynamic balance, particularly in the deep foreshortening. He even gave up work on it for several months during the summer of 1964, but when he returned to it in the fall he was able to bring it swiftly to conclusion. He deliberately chose a difficult aspect of a difficult movement. The action of skating is an "unnatural" one and Colville intensified this by showing the figure wearing speed rather than figure skates. Speed skates, with their longer and thinner blades, demand a greater stretching action to shift the skater's weight efficiently from one skate to the other. He shows her at that point in the movement when balance is most critical, for support of her body is wholly dependent on the dynamic movement of the blade through the ice. He draws an exact equivalence between a difficult action in the three-dimensional world and a demanding pictorial problem; the achievement of the one is parallel to the achievement of the other.

The painting also challenges the conventions for depicting the human figure in action. The history of art can, at one level, be described in terms of conventions that have been developed to depict the human figure, and through these conventions meaning has been expressed like a language of gestures. This language is not simply a matter of anatomically "correct" drawing, but of introducing tensions that imply movement and hence imitate life. Colville has described these conventions by contrasting the painting of animals and human beings:

> The shapes of animals are very interesting ... [but] the human shape one recognizes as being set. You can't do just anything with it because [as] we are human, we identify more with what is done with a human shape.[3]

We can compare Colville's challenge in *Skater* to Sir Henry Raeburn's *Reverend Robert Walker Skating* (fig. 16), where Raeburn carefully compromises the movements of skating to maintain the gentleman's dignity.

Swimmer 1962
Egg tempera
53.3 x 71.1 cm
Dr. Helen J. Dow
Catalogue Raisonné No. 67

Berlin Bus 1978
Acrylic polymer emulsion
53.4 x 53.4 cm
Private Collection, Montreal
Catalogue Raisonné No. 112

fig. 16
Sir Henry Raeburn (Scottish, 1756-1823)
Reverend Robert Walker Skating c. 1784
Oil on canvas
76.2 x 63.5 cm
National Galleries of Scotland, Edinburgh

Colville's picture recalls Paul Klee's observation that we continue "to stand despite all possibility of falling." Klee meant that in spite of the infinite possibilities we can imagine, the world as we know it does exist; its set of circumstances prevails. It is a view of life's tenuous relativity that Klee expressed in scores of works where balance depends on the slimmest of threads. Colville manifests the relativity of balance from a totally different direction, showing that no matter how difficult "standing" may be, it must be made substantial and convincing. Even if the image of *Skater* presses balance to the limits, he seeks to stabilize it through an illusion of reality. He does this not only through the virtuosity of his drawing in perspective, but also by the powerful geometry of the picture. He fixes the figure in the frame with the ends of the skate blades touching its edges so that the right blade holds and balances the off-centred position of the left, which lies directly below the crown of the woman's head.

Skater is an analogue of balance between the "real-world" subject and the reality of the painting. In contrast, *Swimming Race* of 1958 (CR 58) appears to loosen that relationship because it seems that the action must be resolved outside the picture itself; the swimmer closest to us, for instance, would already be beyond the frame of the picture by the time she hit the water. But the painting is not part of a narrative; the totality of its meaning is contained within its frame. That meaning is concerned with overlapping descriptions of time co-existing in a single moment. It opens up that moment to show us action not as a sequence, but as a series of simultaneously existing layers.

Each of the swimmers, at a different point in the dive, represents one aspect of control. In this way (recalling the medieval pictorial device in which one figure is depicted in several different places within a single picture), the subject of the picture is concerned with change as it is implied through one critical moment; once the swimmer has shifted her weight to a certain point her drop into the water is unstoppable, her action becomes inevitable. But the action itself is one of control, she must bring about the dive in a safe and efficient manner.

Colville likes to repeat the story of Jung talking with James Joyce. Jung, who was treating Joyce's daughter, said, "It's like your daughter is falling into deeper and deeper water"; to which Joyce replied, "But that's what I do everytime I write." The last word, however, was with Jung, "Ah, but you're diving and she's falling."[4] The story does not describe this picture, but it does underline the conditions of control over the inevitable processes of action, control which exists even when we cannot exactly predict the outcome of the steps that are taken. We cannot predict because we do not know the future, but we must develop our abilities so as to come to terms with those uncertainties that face us.

The picture combines secure elements with others that are not precisely known. The enclosure of the pool on the right is countered by the open water on the left. And our place as spectators, set somewhere insecurely close to the edge, is opposed by the tightly bound limits of the pool on the far side, with its enclosing fence and ladders leading out of the pool. Our viewpoint, however, is secure. It lies level with the horizontal bar of the boundary fence and meets the eye-level of the swimmer furthest away from us. From there our eyes follow the diagonal formed by the swimmers' heads. Each of the girls is a little more advanced in her dive, the face of each one progressively obscured. On the far side stands a man with a starting pistol and stopwatch, controlling the swimming race. He initiates the event and through his timing of it implies its closure. He marks an external

Prize Cow 1977
Serigraph, edition 70
43.0 cm diameter
Mira Godard Gallery
Catalogue Raisonné No. 139

Church and Horse 1964
Acrylic polymer emulsion
55.3 x 68.5 cm
The Montreal Museum of Fine Arts,
    Purchase, Horsley and Annie Townsend
    Bequest and Anonymous Donor
Catalogue Raisonné No. 71

control, just as the movements of the swimmers predict their individual control over their actions. In a number of aspects he recalls the traditional emblem of time personified as Father Time, invariably represented as an old man carrying the attributes of a scythe and an hourglass; here he is brought into the twentieth century equipped with a pistol and a watch. The painting becomes an allegory of our existence in time, showing what we can control and what we cannot.

In these paintings of the late 1950s and early 1960s – *Athletes*, *Child Skipping*, *Skater*, *Swimming Race* – Colville describes moments of extreme physical activity, which make us aware of time through split-second suspension of action. He chooses moments that are not only crucial for success but also most demanding in terms of balance and equilibrium. Yet these moments are not taken *from* time, they are *within* time. It is a theme he has followed in a number of subsequent pictures, with overlapping actions and memories and associations. To see how this theme has developed and expanded in terms of its implications for meaning, we must move forward to 1978 to look at what is to my mind one of the most compelling of Colville's pictures, *Berlin Bus* (CR 112).

This picture arose directly from the time in 1971 that he spent in Berlin as Visiting Artist under the *Berliner Kunstlerprogramm*. He was offered a year's stay, but accepted the invitation for only six months, because he did not want to be away from his studio for longer than that. He made one painting there *The River Spree* (CR 87) and many drawings, some of which formed the basis for *Berlin Bus* and the major serigraph *Morning* of 1981 (CR 144). Accepting the invitation was also difficult for him because he had to come to terms with being in Germany. It was the first time he had been there since the war and he was both curious and uncertain as to what his reaction would be. Such feelings were heightened by the fact that the invitation was to Berlin, once the centre of Nazi power and now divided between symbols of its destruction in East Berlin and of Western materialism in West Berlin. It is a place whose past and present are filled with the fact and threat of violence.

One of the things that quickly caught his interest in Berlin were the double-decked buses. He took a long series of photographs of these vehicles from every angle, stationary and in movement, including some night-time shots. The combination of one of these buses and the notary's sign, *Notar*, with figures walking on the street, was the subject of one of the Berlin drawings (fig. 17). Later in 1971, on his return to Canada, he took up the idea of combining the figure of the running girl with the double-decked bus and a night-time setting. Seven years passed before he took the idea up again and followed it through to the painting.

Swimming Race 1958
Oil and synthetic resin
60.9 x 98.5 cm
National Gallery of Canada, Ottawa
Catalogue Raisonné No. 58

Heron 1977
Serigraph, edition 70
33.0 x 86.0 cm
Mira Godard Gallery
Catalogue Raisonné No. 138

Cat and Artist 1979
Serigraph, edition 70
23.1 cm diameter
Mira Godard Gallery
Catalogue Raisonné No. 142

fig. 17
Study for Berlin Bus July 10, 1971
Ink
18.2 x 13.0 cm
Collection the artist

His first drawing of the subject in 1978 was reminiscent of *Horse and Train*, with a girl running for a bus in a composition of deep and plunging perspective (fig. 18). He soon revised this to bring the girl and the bus in parallel (fig. 19) and the remainder of the series of drawings refined this approach. All the elements of the picture were brought more or less parallel with the picture plane: the notary sign, the girl, the lamp standard, the bus, and the houses on the far side of the street. The viewpoint he takes is low, as if he were sitting in a car or at a café table, an angle that increases the impression of speed and exertion of the girl's pose.

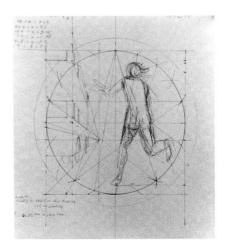

fig. 18
Study for Berlin Bus January 18, 1978
Pencil and ink
29.6 x 20.7 cm
Collection the artist

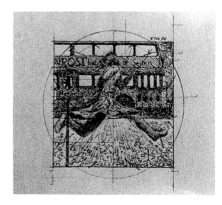

fig. 19
Study for Berlin Bus February 5, 1978
Pencil and ink
30.3 x 22.7 cm
Collection the artist

Even though it was developed from superficially banal ideas – a girl running for the bus, a woman pushing a pram along a street, a bus passing behind – the picture is disturbing. Most of all the girl seems out of place. Her clothing is more suited to the sports field or boating club and her sprinting action is extravagant – somehow even violent – in the context of a city street. The sense of being out of place is heightened as we try to reconcile her with the setting. Does she run parallel to the other elements, or is she trapped by them and seeking escape? Her open and strained form contrasts with the other tightly drawn, rectilinear, and closed elements. We cannot say whether the bus is moving, but if it were its motion would be smooth and effortless. Only one thing breaks the tautness of the picture: the witty opposition between the straining action of the girl and the "on-guard" stance of the bear on the notary's sign.

If the girl seems out of place (out of step), what of the other elements in the picture? In at least three ways there are references to the notion of conveying – the orderly transfer of something from one place to another. First, the bus obviously is a conveyance, carrying people from point to point. Second, there is the reference to a notary in the sign. A notary is a legal officer who specializes in conveyancing, that is in carrying title – say to land or other property – from one person to another. The third notion of conveying comes through the sign on the side of the bus. This would read in full *"[Berliner] Morgenpost hat viele gute Seiten,"* which means literally "The Berlin Morning Post [a daily newspaper] has many good pages," but which implies a range of meanings; "Seite" means also "sides" in the sense of facets, and in English we could extend this to mean "taking sides" or expressing an opinion.

These three elements, notary, bus, advertisement, are all embodiments of social and institutional values. The maintenance of the structure of modern society depends on the orderly and regulated conveyance of goods, services, and people, whether in transport, the law, or in the communication of information and opinion. Between these the girl runs with a frantic nightmarish energy, as if trying to break free from some unnameable threat. It is as if she alone is aware of something terrible, of a world whose order and efficiency, marked even in the precise placing of the paving stones, could at any moment split apart.

The Berlin setting is precisely relevant. The long period over which Colville thought about the subject is itself a sign of the difficulty in finding the right terms for it. It was, perhaps, only with that distance that he could fully recognize how his personal responses to being in Germany could reflect a wider situation. The painting has strong political overtones. The history of Germany, the destruction and restoration through the "German miracle," is nowhere more sharply felt than in Berlin. Physically, in the western part, it has been almost totally rebuilt – only the tower of the Kaiser-Wilhelm-Gedächtsnis-Kirche stands to mark the devastation in 1945; in the eastern sector, many buildings have been left as they were at the end of the war. West Berlin has become a showplace of revival and Western materialism and a symbol of opposition to the East, underwritten by President Kennedy's 1962 declaration, "Ich bin ein Berliner." Yet it is a place whose violent past carries into an uncertain present. As a city sliced in half and set deep inside the German Democratic Republic, it has been in recent years the focus of social and political unrest.

To speak of the picture this way is not to exclude other levels of meaning, although Colville is conscious of his recent work reflecting strong political content. Without negating that aspect, the nightmarish character of the picture cuts into levels at which all of us exist. It is like the way that a dream breaks through the rationalizing structure of the conscious, serving to show how we exist constantly at different levels of reality. The fact that the girl here is "out of place" is relative only to the expectations we construct for our conscious and everyday levels. The dream world is no less real, carrying its own time and space, which, if different from the objective world, is in no way rendered invalid by it.

The painting may carry several levels of meaning simultaneously because it determines, poetically, its own structure of time and space. Through Colville's precise realism this structure responds to the time and space of the real world, bringing the image into terms that relate directly to our experience. But the painting may also be seen to compress objective reality into a time and space that exists only subjectively. In the same way that a word or phrase in a poem can, by its context, carry multiple readings and interfold several levels, so also a form, shape, or colour in a picture can open onto a range of interpretations. The precise manner in which representational forms are shaped and disposed within the picture opens up meanings that exist within the reality of the painting alone. It is this independent casting of reality that allows us to carry together both political and dream-like readings of *Berlin Bus*.

Just as *Berlin Bus* seems to cast back in a number of ways to *Horse and Train*, the two pictures can be further linked by an intervening work, the 1964 painting *Church and Horse* (CR 71). Like them, this one is reduced to a few clearly defined elements – church, horse, fence, monument – and similarly demands our attention to the precise relationships among them. Also like the other two pictures, the site is precisely chosen and described. The church is the United Church at Hastings outside Amherst, Nova Scotia. It is a tiny building, standing back from an unpaved road and set on the edge of high ground. The wooden fence that stood at the time Colville painted the picture has since been removed.

The compositional structure is simple; the church and fence stand parallel to the picture plane (and the roadway); the monument, horse, and gate are placed diagonally to the picture plane. As with *Horse and Train* and *Berlin Bus* we are presented with a situation that, if improbable, is not impossible. The spectator's viewpoint is low, as so frequently in Colville's work, as if one were sitting in a car. This low, frontal viewpoint gives the church an impressive but somewhat forbidding aspect, a point ironically underlined by the plaque attached to it, which reads at the bottom, "Everyone Welcome." The fence and monument, too, seem to indicate restrictions; it is against these that the horse, galloping and unbridled, is set. The horse represents the animal world, united with ours in the process of life and death, but totally indifferent to the structures and organizations by which we seek to face the facts of our existence. It is not a surrealistic event that we see in the picture, but a reflection of the reality of our own world, a reality as commonplace as it is fundamental. The surprise association of horse and church is a poetic device that heightens this meaning, drawing it out of the conventions and expectations of the everyday. As in *Berlin Bus* the structure of time and space belongs to the painting alone, but the authenticity of the elements brings the image directly and in an unnerving way into the context of the everyday world.

To speak of authenticity – and it has arisen many times already – is to step carefully along the edge of the issue of painting and photography as it affects Colville's work. Colville recognizes that for many people this appears to be an important issue, but in fact the use of photography has played a relatively small part in the development of his work. There have been three periods in his career when Colville has used photography as an active component in constructing his pictures. The first was during the war and the second when he was in Berlin in 1971. In both instances the purpose was a means to store information – but on neither occasion did he find, in the end, that it had been helpful. The third occasion has been in recent years. He was intrigued by the development of the SX70 camera, and bought one in 1977. He has used it in the studio in developing such pictures as *Berlin Bus*, *Dog and Priest*, *Morning*, and *Night Walk* (CR 112, 113, 144 and 120). The use of the Polaroid camera has been wholly pragmatic: to fix particular poses, particularly when he uses himself as the model. These photographs come at a late stage in the development of a composition, as a check on the chosen pose in relation to the geometric scheme he has designed for the picture. Its use is mechanical rather than conceptual.

Colville's relative lack of interest in photography has not been from any purist motives. He underlines his admiration for the American artist Thomas Eakins, a pioneer in the use of photography in relation to painting. It is simply that he has not found that the technique suited his approach:

> Photographs tend not to give me the information I want, and *do* give me information I *don't* want.... I think this has also something to do with *memory*; it is important for me to be able to forget some things. As an observer who sometimes draws from life.... I can be a filter; the camera takes everything, forgets nothing, and cannot *touch* or really *measure*.[5]

Nevertheless Colville's work has not escaped comparison to photography, sometimes disparaging, as when Richard Cork, the English critic, wrote of the paintings being glorified photographs;[6] and sometimes presumably by way of compliment, as in Patrick Hutchings' description of *Hound in Field* (CR 56): "there is no anthropomorphic anguish in the dog's eye. He is closer to a Kodachrome than a Landseer."[7] The whole issue of photography and painting has changed radically in recent years, with an explosion of interest in photography and the development of new critical interest in its relationship to painting. Colville's views, too, seem to have shifted a little in recent years.

> It was only maybe ten years ago that I realized that Eakins had used photographs. People always ask me if I paint from photographs and in the layman's mind it seems an absolutely key issue. And it is an important issue. I have sometimes wondered if the use of photographs, which I have done since around 1977 or so, reflects a kind of formal change.[8]

His present use of photography is primarily as an aid at a specific point in the process of a work, rather than a point of departure in the inventive development of a picture. His views on memory and forgetting remain unaltered, as does his distinction between *making* and *taking*. In a statement in 1967 he wrote:

> It is important to realize that a photograph is *taken* whereas a painting is *made*. To *take* something is a form of abduction ... whereas to *make* something as an artist is ... a kind of love-making – that is, it is only worthwhile to *make* that which one loves, respects, reveres or is captivated by.[9]

In some ways, Colville's interest has been drawn more toward movies than still photography. *In the Woods* (CR 109) was directly inspired from seeing the movie *The Conformist*; and he realized after the fact that *Ravens at the Dump* (CR 130) derived from a wartime newsreel. His interest is not concerned with the narrative structure of film, but with the visual relationships between the stilled moment in each frame and the sense of movement in the sequence. It is the consequence of movement that carries with it the emotional or moral or political overtones.

The relationship of Colville's work to photography may seem incongruous with his adherence to a painterly structure rooted in the traditions of the Renaissance. But the apparent contradiction reflects directly on a fundamental aspect of his make-up, an essential conservatism in values and combined with an acceptance of the circumstances of modern life, with its technological growth. The evidence of his interest in technology and its implications for our society runs right through his work, standing side by side with the values of human relationships or the parallel world of animals.

Colville stands heir to the Renaissance canon of painting in three ways. He insists on the relationship between serious subject matter and correct formal organization; on the importance of a direct relationship between pictorial representation and our experience of the natural world; and on communication of meaning through movement. In the pictures we have looked at in this chapter I have emphasized those with a strong sense of movement, where the actions of running, swimming, jumping, and skating are presented in such a way as to heighten our appreciation of the relationship between the boundaries of time and space. The pictorial structure that Colville develops, for all its realism, is relevant above all to a precise reading of the painting itself. It is through this structure that he can open the pictures out to multiple levels of interpretation.

My Father With His Dog 1968
Acrylic polymer emulsion
93.6 cm diameter
Private Collection, Ottobrunn, West
    Germany
Catalogue Raisonné No. 79

FIVE

THE ARTIST AS A
RESPONSIBLE MAN

The two works of fiction that have most deeply impressed Colville have been Ford Madox Ford's *Parade's End* and John dos Passos' *USA* trilogy. Together they form an interesting combination of perspectives; Ford's book is written from the viewpoint of the English upper classes around the time of World War I, and dos Passos' is a quintessentially American view of the first thirty years of the twentieth century. Dos Passos was an American who knew Europe well, and Ford an Englishman who spent the last years of his life in self-imposed exile in France and the United States. Colville has always been sensitive, in a positive way, to the combination of British roots and American cultural influence. It reflects his own background and the roots from which his art developed, first under the influence of Stanley Royle and then through his interest in American art.

Colville was drawn to these two books in response to that sensitivity. In addition they both deal with the period of his parents' generation, and they are sustained treatments of interwoven levels of time – the lives of individuals are swept up in the distortion of war and the pressures of social change. Both of these aspects express Colville's own compelling fascination with time:

> I'm...very conscious of the passage of time. I've always been very conscious of [it], even when I was young.[1]

He has reflected this preoccupation in his work in many ways, including a special sensitivity to the process of aging. This concern is not a mark of morbidity, but of reality, nowhere more forcefully made than in the recent painting *Target Pistol and Man* (CR 117). This picture makes an interesting parallel with the portrait of his father, *My Father With His Dog* (CR 79), that he had made twelve years before. Colville reflects in this picture, and in others which have older men as subjects, his respect for seniority.

My Father With His Dog is unusual because it was made as a portrait. Driving away one day from a visit to his father, Colville looked back to see him standing on the steps of his house and was struck by the realization that he was an old man, someone whose life and hopes lay essentially behind him. It seemed vital for Colville to preserve that image of him. The low viewpoint of the picture responds both to that of the artist sitting in a car and the level of a child approaching the house. The painting thus gently relates the past and the present, Colville's childhood memories of his father and the realization of his aging. At this point the old man was living alone in his Amherst home with his dog, his life "a complete and hermetic world."[2] Colville paints this aspect not by seeking to penetrate it, but by accepting and respecting it. The painting is concerned with dignity, not with psychology, nor with pressing transcendent symbolism (father/

fig. 20
Ben Shahn (American, 1898-1969)
The Riveter
Tempera on paperboard
83.8 x 38.1 cm
University of Maryland Art Gallery

Father), but with a simple respect for the man's integrity and independence. Colville does not try to record his father's specific achievements or disappointments, but marks the process of life, which is a process of growing old.

In many ways, some overt and some subtle, Colville's *oeuvre* shows many debts to his father. The work his father had done in steel construction is echoed, for instance, by the steel frame bridges in *August, High Diver*, and *Dog and Bridge*, (CR 73, 125, and 107) and the workers in *Two Riveters* (CR 46). The latter is a sketch rather than a finished painting, intended, perhaps, to be developed further. It was influenced by a Ben Shahn painting (fig. 20), part of his *Resources of America* of 1938, a mural in the New York Central Postal Station in the Bronx. Colville's picture differs from Shahn's by introducing a second figure. Although both men are working on the structure – we can see two safety-harness loops slung over the upright on the left – only one of the men seems to be actively engaged. The other, whom Colville appears characteristically to have modelled on himself, coincides with our viewpoint, presenting the duality of the observer and the observed. The reference in the subject matter to his father is evident and, in part, a dedication to him in his sixty-fifth year. It was through his father's work that Colville was able to receive a sound education and follow the profession he had chosen.

Colville is very aware of his father's disappointments. Colville Senior had grown up in a small coal-mining town in Scotland where Colville's grandfather had been a carter and supplied pit ponies for use in the mines. Colville's father had inherited an interest in horses, but in Canada was never able to follow it in any professional way. Colville recalls:

> We always went to the Winter Fair in Amherst and I found it very moving. My parents would come with us … my father had come from the country in Scotland and had … [borne] the brunt of the transfer from an agrarian to an industrial [life].… He had this immense, unexpressed longing to be something like a doctor or veterinarian, not doing what he was doing. I remember sitting beside him at the Fair and he would identify [the] horses. This is part of the vicarious business of seeing something through someone else's eyes or experience.[3]

Colville reflects this vicarious interest in pictures like *Three Horses*, *Horse and Train*, and *Church and Horse* (CR 16, 43, and 71).

My Father With His Dog was therefore a special picture both in subject matter and occasion, but he approached the subject of older men in other paintings with an equivalent sensitivity. The earliest of these is the 1953 painting *Man on Verandah* (CR 37) where the man is

Two Riveters 1954
Casein tempera
50.8 x 38.1 cm
University of Guelph Collection, Macdonald
   Stewart Art Centre, Gift of the Ontario
   Veterinary College Alumni Association,
   1972
Catalogue Raisonné No. 46

August 1964
Acrylic polymer emulsion
43.1 x 86.3 cm
Private Collection, Ottawa
Catalogue Raisonné No. 73

Man on Verandah 1953
Glazed tempera
38.1 x 50.8 cm
Collection G.H. Southam
Catalogue Raisonné No. 37

modelled on Rhoda Colville's step-father. As in the portrait of his father, Colville does not seek to interpret the man's expression, or to try to persuade us of what he is thinking – he has often said that he is not interested in personality. The value of the picture lies in its naturalness, in the gentle dignity of the man, in the simple act of the cat cleaning her paw, in the boats riding their anchors on the tide. The painting is invested quietly with the flow of natural events into which made-made structures – the verandah, the table and chair, the boats – intervene, but neither slow nor divert the flow. The mood of the picture seems to parallel some lines of T.S. Eliot's "The Dry Salvages," a superb passage on growing older:

> It seems, as one becomes older,
> That the past has another pattern, and ceases to be a mere
>   sequence –
> . . . .
> We had the experience but missed the meaning,
> And approach to the meaning restores the experience
> In a different form, beyond any meaning
> We can assign to happiness.[4]

Similar to *Man on Verandah* in its sensitivity to older men is *Mr. Wood in April* of 1960 (CR 63), a painting of particularly fine and delicate handling. The man in the painting is shown walking past the wrought iron fence fronting his house, a property now the official residence of the president of Mount Allison University. Like *Man on Verandah* this picture establishes a relationship by setting the man between the man-made and the natural. The fence with its stone uprights and ornate ironwork echoes the trees, its firmly drawn design contrasting with the soft glow of colour that arises from the swelling leaf buds. Both pictures place the men, with their reflections on a lifetime's experience, in a context that unites the everyday and the larger rhythms of nature, the tides, and the seasons.

In two other pictures Colville made of older men, *Ocean Limited* and *Professor of Romance Languages* (CR 65 and 91), the people were neither relations nor acquaintances. In both instances, although he had little personal contact with the two men, they were familiar figures to him within the context of his own life. Colville, in his daily routine of walking or driving along Main Street in Wolfville would see "the professor" on his own daily walk. The setting of the picture has him passing the Acadia University playing field, behind which is the university's central heating plant. It seems to link two aspects of the academic life, the abstract one of ideas and knowledge, the practical one of the mechanics of institutional life – and with a wry sense of humour. In addition there is the coincidence of everyday routines, of

High Diver 1957
Serigraph, edition 20
99.5 x 44.4 cm
Catalogue Raisonné No. 125

Mr. Wood in April 1960
Oil and synthetic resin
60.9 x 91.4 cm
Mr. and Mrs. J.W. Black
Catalogue Raisonné No. 63

Professor of Romance Languages 1973
Acrylic polymer emulsion
68.5 x 91.4 cm
Mr. & Mrs. Irving Ungerman
Catalogue Raisonné No. 91

observing someone without really knowing him but being, in a physical way, constantly aware of his life.

This sense of observation, stressing the feeling of being an outsider, is underlined in a group of pictures showing people working. His emphasis is on those involved in physical occupations, and by painting them he links their activity with his own, whether a snowplow operator in the serigraph of the 1967 *Snowplow* (CR 131); a road roller operator in *Road Work* of 1969 (CR 80); a man and a boy making milk deliveries in *Milk Truck* of 1959 (CR 60); or a gas station attendant in *Truck Stop* of 1966 (CR 75). There is a clear continuity in these works with his wartime art, in which he so often chose to show soldiers with the machinery of war, particularly transport vehicles, trucks, tanks, landing craft, warships, and aircraft. As I pointed out earlier, Colville was acutely aware of being in the war but professionally distanced from it. And he is also sensitive to the physical activity of work – again perhaps a reflection on the lives of his parents. There is a real response to this in the very way he does his own work. The techniques he uses are demanding and the process slow and meticulous, not only in painting but in observing, researching, drawing, and planning.

He has spoken, in relation to *Snowplow,* of a sense of envy felt by the standing man observing the man who drives the plow.[5] And further, he identifies the plowdriver in a rather surprising way:

> In a way the driver of the *Snowplow* is my friend Charles Forsyth, the United Church Minister who is now [1967] assistant to the Premier of New Brunswick, or he is also Strelniker in Pasternak's *Dr Zhivago* in his armoured train.[6]

It is a curious form of identification, separating the notion of the observer/artist from the man of action. He identifies the principal model as someone involved both in organized religion and in government; the snowplow is literally and figuratively an instrument of action. Colville was explicit on this point: "The lettering on the snowplow, 'Department of Public Works, New Brunswick', gives the hint of the theme."[7] This theme is of involvement, of people participating in public events. There are, within our society, clearly defined places for those actions, whether in politics, in the church, or in keeping the roads open. Colville reflects on his position as a person involved in physical work but before that an observer.

His attitude to work is expressed in a different way in the 1969 painting *Road Work* (CR 80). The painting contrasts road building with the brilliantly described landscape beyond. By emphasizing the penetration of the road into the countryside, he makes the serene quality of the distinct view all the more important. We must reconcile these two aspects, our respect for the landscape itself, and our

Snowplow 1967
Serigraph, edition 20
61.0 x 81.2 cm
Catalogue Raisonné No. 131

Milk Truck 1959
Oil and synthetic resin
45.7 x 45.7 cm
C-I-L Inc.
Catalogue Raisonné No. 60

Truck Stop 1966
Acrylic polymer emulsion
91.4 x 91.4 cm
Museum Ludwig, Köln
Catalogue Raisonné No. 75

acceptance of the intrusion into it, which is both a product and a metaphor of our society. The young man with the sign reflects this reconciliation. His view of the landscape is greater than ours, and the sign he leans on has the "SLOW" side towards us, but the red of his vest implies the "STOP" on the other side. Against this figure moves the ponderous road-roller, its colour echoing the "SLOW" sign.

The type of layering that we find in these pictures, the engagement of personal references, and the device of the observer reflect Colville's view of the artist's position. He is conscious of his observation of and his debt to others, and the fact that his paintings are frequently concerned with the world of action is, in a sense, a way of returning his own occupation back to that world. He described this responsibility early in his career:

> In my opinion, painting should neither be fun nor primarily a means of self-expression. I regard paintings as things produced not to relieve the artist, not to serve him, but to serve other people who will look at them; a cabinet-maker does not construct a chair in order to sit down on it himself. Thus I regard art not as a means of soliloquizing, but as a means of communication.[8]

Colville has never questioned the fact that the business of the artist is to find the ways in which serious ideas can be clearly communicated without false nostalgia, sentimentality, or mawkishness. This consciousness of the role of the artist, in the observation of others and in the responsibility of communication, is nowhere more strongly felt than in the 1966 painting *Truck Stop* (CR 75).

This picture, as Robert Melville has pointed out, recalls Edward Hopper's 1940 painting *Gas* (fig. 21).[9] The paintings have in common their contrast between twilight settings and artificial lighting, and the sense of an isolated island of modern civilization set in a desolate stretch of highway. But the presentation of the paintings, particularly as they reflect the positions of the artists, are markedly different. The mystery in Hopper's picture is substantially a result of its detached viewpoint. The spectator is a concealed watcher, a spy whose suspended threat is echoed in the dark stand of trees that close round the gas station. The perspective of Colville's picture is quite different. The viewpoint is low, as if the spectator is the truck driver who has jumped down to stretch his legs. The attention of the gas-pump attendant is directed toward us, involving us immediately in the action. Between us and the attendant are the dog and truck, which together form one of Colville's most extraordinary passages of painterly virtuosity. Their contrasting textures would be difficult under any circumstances, but they are fiercely so on the shadowed side of conflicting light sources.

fig. 21
Edward Hopper (American, 1882-1967)
Gas 1940
Oil on canvas
66.7 x 102.2 cm
Collection The Museum of Modern Art,
   New York, Mrs. Simon Guggenheim Fund

The picture is built on the junction of two axes; the attendant addressing the driver/artist/spectator directs his attention at right angles to the truck; the dog placed diagonally to this grid asserts its independent interests. The lurid artificial light provokes a curious visual echo between the cast on the man's arm, with its looped sling, and the form of the gas pump. More than that, a narrative reading of the picture (that the truck has pulled in for a fill-up) is difficult because of the position of the truck relative to the pump. The attendant's job of filling the tank is made almost impossible; he suffers, it seems, a double disability and we, in part, seem to be responsible. If the spectator in Hopper's *Gas* is in a privileged position, we here, even in the shadows, are open to the address – perhaps the complaint – of the attendant. Colville has spoken of a person observing often being the subject of suspicion[10] and this picture seems to make us the source of threat and discomfort and not the dog, who is indifferent to our presence. The truck, for all its massiveness, is no barrier to the attendant's questioning or reproach.

In *Truck Stop* the sense of communication is frontal and direct, but in other pictures such as *Dog, Boy and School Bus* of 1960 (CR 62) it is divided. This painting has sometimes been described in terms of aggression; as if the dog were attacking the boy. To my mind quite the opposite is the case. The relationship between the dog and boy is one of welcome and of mutual affection; the dog licks the boy's face, the boy puts out his arm to clasp the dog. Colville describes a relationship which is both spontaneous and profound. The gestures of dog and boy, expressing their private communication, project a warmth that

Road Work 1969
Acrylic polymer emulsion
53.3 x 83.6 cm
Mr. & Mrs. Jules Loeb
Catalogue Raisonné No. 80

One Swallow 1980
Acrylic polymer emulsion
33.0 x 40.8 cm
From the Collection of Mrs. John Rykert
Catalogue Raisonné No. 116

Dog, Boy and School Bus 1960
Oil and synthetic resin
68.5 x 59.3 cm
Private Collection
Catalogue Raisonné No. 62

encloses them from the coldness of the day and the gloomy lowering skies. They are set within a context filled with references to means of public communication; the mail box, the telephone poles, the bus are objective devices for communication. Yet none of these, singly or collectively, can weigh against the intensity of the unspoken bond between the boy and the dog. Their relationship is beyond conventional language and the means by which those are carried, a point clearly made in the structure of the picture. The perspective sets the mail box, the telephone poles, and the bus on a path of convergence toward a vanishing point where the road and horizon meet. This is the point toward which our eyes are drawn, above the heads of the boy and dog, the viewpoint of an adult. Locked in their own communication, the boy and the dog see at that moment only as far as each other. We can see further, but how much have we lost?

Animals and the animal world have always played an important role in Colville's life. He has, since childhood, always kept animals and it is inconceivable to him that he would not have animals as part of his household, so it is most natural that animals should take a prominent place in his work. Nearly one-third of his paintings and half of his serigraphs have animals either as their main subject or as a significant part in the image. With the exception of birds, the animals are always domestic – dogs, cats, cows, bulls, and sheep. Paintings and serigraphs of wild animals are restricted to birds – the crow, the raven, the hawk, the owl, the heron – with the emphasis on the larger hunting, scavenging, or carrion-eating birds. In just one picture, *One Swallow* (CR 116), does he paint an insect-eater.

Colville has underscored the importance of animals in his life and his work many times:

> I saw an article by a woman in a religious commune in which she said they had three rules, no liquor, no drugs, and no dogs. I thought this was very strange, because to me the presence of animals seems absolutely necessary. I feel that without animals everything is incomplete.[11]

And in discussion with Helen Dow he said,

> I think of animals as being incapable of evil, and I certainly don't think this about people. The idea of a bad dog is absolutely inconceivable to me, unless it has been driven crazy by people.[12]

Colville's attitude toward animals corresponds in many ways to that of Paul Klee, whose love of animals is so often reflected in his work. Klee spoke of being envious of animals, contrasting their lives against the

Running Dog 1968
Serigraph, edition 43
35.2 x 61.0 cm
Mira Godard Gallery
Catalogue Raisonné No. 132

Woman and Terrier 1963
Acrylic polymer emulsion
60.9 cm diameter
Private Collection
Catalogue Raisonné No. 70

essentially tragic nature of human beings. In animals he saw a unity among all aspects of their lives. The human being, however, is afflicted by a tragic gap, the gap between his physical rooting in the world and his yearning to transcend it. It is the penalty of consciousness that we can recognize both our objective and subjective states. Animals enjoy a wholeness, a state of grace, because their existence is at one with their limitations whereas we, aware of our limitations, are spurred by that knowledge to discontent.[13] Klee's contemporary, the poet Rainer Maria Rilke, noted a similar contrast near the opening of the first of the *Duino Elegies*:

> Oh, who is there
> to prevail upon? Neither angels nor men,
> and already the ingenious beasts are aware –
> that we are not reliably at home
> in our interpreted world.[14]

For Colville the animal world stands as an example both of the notion of wholeness and of the acceptance of limitations. He has spoken of limitations as being freedom, that our ability to act demands an appreciation of the context within which freedom can be exercised. It is this sense of limitation and freedom that is so finely expressed in the serigraph *Running Dog* (CR 132) of 1968. The wire-haired terrier bounds across the playing field, indifferent to the grid markings placed there for football. The dog's sense of play has a freedom that we can barely imagine, for even in our recreation we organize and determine our actions according to rules. If that picture expresses the animal's sense of freedom, a slightly earlier serigraph, *Cat on Fence* (CR 124), shows the animal's ability to sense its capacities and limitations. The natural sense of balance and care in the cat's movement is tested as it walks along the fence. The narrowness of the barrier presents no problem to the cat because its precise movements and innate senses are balanced to the task it undertakes.

Colville's sympathy toward animals is reflected in his brilliantly observed studies of their forms and actions. I have mentioned that he feels a freedom with the shapes of animals which is not possible with the human figure; his *Two Pacers* (CR 26) is an example of this, as is the serigraph *Dog with Bone* of 1961 (CR 128). One of his finest depictions of the sheer beauty of animal movement comes in the 1958 painting *Hound in Field* (CR 56). Colville's ability to fix the dog's sense of balance in movement must stand as one of the great examples of animal painting. He has an acute sense of the balance and disposition of the animal, which is all the more remarkable because for this picture he did not make his customary geometric drawings. Colville said of this picture that its formation seemed to come out "like magic."

Hound in Field 1958
Casein tempera
76.2 x 101.6 cm
National Gallery of Canada, Ottawa
Catalogue Raisonné No. 56

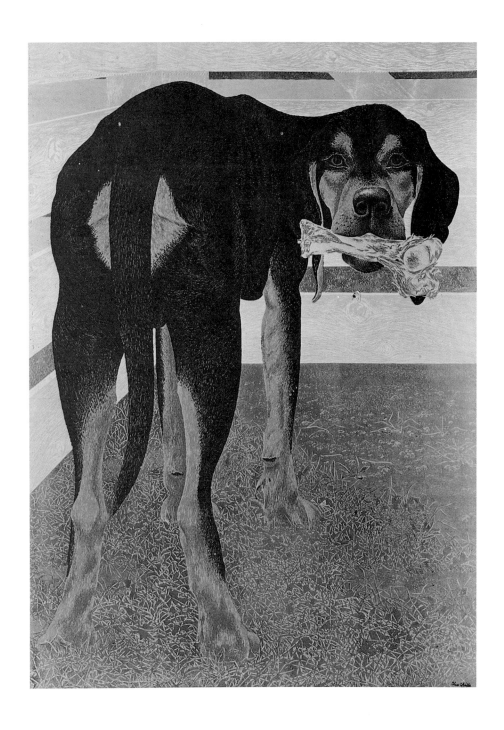

Dog with Bone 1960-61
Serigraph, edition 20
75.9 x 53.3 cm
Catalogue Raisonné No. 128

Cat on Fence 1956
Serigraph, edition 20
53.3 x 71.1 cm
Catalogue Raisonné No. 124

Cow and Calf 1969
Acrylic polymer emulsion
40.0 x 53.3 cm
Private Collection, Düsseldorf, West
   Germany
Catalogue Raisonné No. 81

Moon and Cow 1963
Oil and synthetic resin
68.5 x 91.4 cm
Donnelley Erdman, Aspen, Colorado
Catalogue Raisonné No. 68

Backdrop for Vesper Service 1954
Casein on wrapping paper
2.44 x 9.75 m
Destroyed
Catalogue Raisonné No. 156

Christopher Pratt, the Newfoundland painter, closely studied the picture and told Colville that he discovered the composition of *Hound in Field* exactly fitted a "whirling circle," a spiral-like figure developed from a Golden Section, and a compositional structure that Colville has frequently used in his pictures. The Golden Section is a mathematical ratio that has had a long and important history in painting, sculpture, and architecture.[15] Discovered by the Greeks in the mid-fifth century BC, it has been called the "divine proportion" because the proportions it describes, found frequently in natural and animal structures, were thought to be an expression of the divine structure of the world. The architect Le Corbusier based his module on the human body set into a Golden Section rectangle divided at the navel. Le Corbusier's module has been one of the mathematical systems on which Colville has frequently based the proportions of his pictures.

Colville shifts his response to the natural alertness and lean energy of the hound which is in contrast to the equally natural slowness and passivity of the cows in the two pictures, *Cow and Calf* of 1969 and *Moon and Cow* of 1963 (CR 81 and 68), which are among his most contemplative works. The sense of unity in the natural world, particularly in *Moon and Cow*, is brilliantly rendered. In this picture the intervention of man – the fence, water container, and hay stall – seems pathetic against the dominant effect in the picture, the unity of the cow and sky. The black and white patterns on the cow's hide and the irregular shape of its body echo the white and dark blue of the sky. It is a relationship we can see but cannot quite grasp, one so large and so clear that it seems to reflect an inevitable design that transcends all distinctions.

When Colville paints human beings with animals he always shows them in attitudes of care; the girl protecting the ambling cows on a country road in *Stop for Cows* (CR 77), the shepherds on duty over their flocks in *Three Shepherds* (CR 50). This unity between people and animals, expressed as a responsibility, describes a fundamental theme for Colville and finds frequent and varied expression in his art. At one time he sketched a plan for a painting related to the subject of the Good Shepherd. It was never carried through but is an important mark of Colville's beliefs as expressed through the relationship between man and animals. The drawing carries clear reference to the Christian theme of Christ's pastoral duty as guardian of the flock. Specifically it relates to the Twenty-Third Psalm, "The Lord is my Shepherd."

Such references raise the issue of the religious connotations in Colville's art, although he has down-played interpretations of his work that describe it in terms of traditional Christian iconography.[16] This does not mean, however, that he rejects outrightly the moral and

Three Shepherds 1955 (Detail)
Casein tempera
53.3 x 71.1 cm
Hallmark Cards Incorporated
Catalogue Raisonné No. 50

Stop for Cows 1967
Acrylic polymer emulsion
60.9 x 91.4 cm
Museum Boymans-van Beuningen,
    Rotterdam, the Netherlands
Catalogue Raisonné No. 77

ethical values on which Christian doctrine is based. The ideas of caring, of responsibility to others, the integration of all aspects of the natural world, are ones in which he explicitly believes and projects in his work. Brought up in a Roman Catholic family, living in a predominantly – if substantially lapsed – Christian society, his values might naturally be expected to reflect those mores, all the more so given his conservatism toward many social and moral issues. Christianity is part of his background and his character, but not the basis for a dogmatic or exclusive interpretation of his work.

This issue is raised particularly by the 1963 painting *Woman and Terrier* (CR 70). As Helen Dow has pointed out, the composition bears a resemblance to some of Raphael's Madonna and Child pictures. Colville has agreed that the geometric structure and tondo (circular) format raises that relationship.[17] But the analogy cannot be pressed too far. I do not accept, for instance, Helen Dow's argument that the Vickers Viscount in the background is a reference to the Holy Dove, the "incorporeal side of life" (the aircraft is, after all, a most material form of transportation). Further Colville's comment, "I thought of it as a kind of Madonna and Child, or 'Holy Terrier' as I sometimes call it"[18] is hardly to be taken as a definition of the picture's meaning.

The fact of the matter is that he frequently brings forward references to other art that draw us to the serious nature of his subject matter. He accepts the relevance of past art because it is the expression of profound beliefs which people have held toward the reality of the world. Colville, as he has made clear from the start of his career, is interested in approaching subject matter that is relevant to the world in which he lives, but still has the capacity to reach the same deep levels that motivated the great art of the past.

This picture relates closely to the *Dog, Boy and School Bus* (CR 62) in the way that it builds a contrast between the events of the everyday world and those aspects of our lives which are supremely real but essentially beyond description. Colville underlines this point in *Woman and Terrier*, as he did in the earlier picture, by expressing it through a human being and an animal. We can empathize with the affection the woman shows, but the sensibility of the dog remains unknowable – we can only project a human sensibility onto it. Thus Colville points to the ineffable character of all essential relationships. It is in this sense that the reference to the Madonna and Child paintings of Raphael arises, for in those the depiction of the relationship between the two figures can do no more than suggest meaning. The very realism with which Colville describes the world is, in an ironic way, in contrast to the intensity of the reality of feeling, which is beyond description.

That we should not attempt to read his pictures in a specifically

fig. 22
Study for River Spree July 10, 1971
Ink
18.2 x 13.0 cm
Collection the artist

Christian way is further clarified by the magnificent 1978 painting *Dog and Priest* (CR 113). There is an obvious reference, in the relationship between the dog and the man, back to *Woman and Terrier*. The watchful head of the dog seems co-existent with that of the man, its black hair and his black suit merge the two into an indivisible unit, and both are quietly at ease in their natural surroundings. Identifying the man as a priest, as someone concerned with the care (the cure) of souls, gives a sharpness and depth to the picture. We cannot *know* what the dog sees of the world, any more than we can *know* anything beyond our world. We may have faith in an existence beyond, but its form (and its fact) is obscured from us. The dog, however, carries the whole of its world with it. Its faith in its master is tangible and its identification with its world is direct and complete. In that way its example is superior to the priest's. Far from giving support to the religious practice of belief, the picture shows the failure of vision, a failure which is set sharply in relief by putting it in parallel with the complete and unquestioning world of animals.

The example of animals in harmony with their circumstances is the subject of several other pictures, like *The River Spree* of 1971 and *Cyclist and Crow* of 1981 (CR 87 and 119). The setting for the former is the River Spree, which winds through the northern sectors of Berlin, passing into East Berlin near the Moltke Bridge. The woman and dog walking beside the river (his initial idea was in reverse to the painting [fig. 22]) move against the direction of the laden barge. The dog is at one with itself, indifferent to the river traffic and the circumstances of the place. Of the woman's attitude we cannot be certain, the arbitrary

The River Spree 1971
Acrylic polymer emulsion
60.0 x 104.0 cm
Museum der moderner Kunst, Vienna
  Leihgabe Sammlung Ludwig/Aachen
Catalogue Raisonné No. 87

Dog and Priest 1978
Acrylic polymer emulsion
52.0 x 90.0 cm
Collection Mr. & Mrs. William Teron
Catalogue Raisonné No. 113

fig. 23
Arnold Böcklin (Swiss, 1827-1901)
Island of the Dead 1880
Oil on wood
74.5 x 122.5 cm
Collection The Metropolitan Museum of Art,
    New York, Reisinger Fund, 1926

cutting removes the possibility of our ability to identify her reactions. With *Cyclist and Crow* Colville parallels the movements of the woman and the bird. But it is a parallel that can last only for a moment; the woman must hold to the road, the bird must follow only its instincts, now knowing of restrictions.

The world of nature is also a place of violence. It is a natural violence, of death in order to live, of the skills of survival. This is the subject of *Sign and Harrier* of 1970 (CR 82) where the beauty of the bird, its magnificent and graceful flying ability, has been developed for its hunting efficiency. Its attribute of remarkable sight is reinforced by the circular form of the painting and the contrast with the sign. The sign is a reflector and its "blindness" reinforces the piercing glare of the harrier's eye. The capacity for violence and aggression in the natural world is turned back onto us; our language and symbols of threat and violence are often drawn from our observations of the animal world.

This point intuitively arose in the serigraph *Ravens at the Dump* (CR 130). The raven has been a symbol, in many cultures, of death. In Jewish legend the bird was originally white but its feathers turned black when it failed to return to the Ark. Its blackness and carrion-eating habits have made it a symbol for the Devil. Colville has said that after he made the image he was struck by how it reminded him of a wartime newsreel he had seen showing a Luftwaffe Heinkel on a bombing mission in Norway.[19]

The most disturbing of all Colville's animal pictures is *Seven Crows* of 1980 (CR 118). He had for some time thought about doing a painting with crows and had made a series of drawings of the birds. He had also been fascinated for many years by a particular setting, a wooded knoll on the far side of a river to the west of Wolfville. His interest in these elements merged through the traditional rhyme,

> One crow sorrow,
> Two crows joy,
> Three crows a letter,
> Four crows a boy,
> Five crows silver,
> Six crows gold,
> Seven crows a story never to be told.

The idea also suggested another image, the painting by the Swiss painter Arnold Böcklin called *Island of the Dead* (fig. 23). Colville has substituted the image of the boat approaching the island for the birds homing on the wood. Their blackness merges into the darkness of the picture and their silent flight contrasts with a deathly stillness in the river and in the depths of the woods.

Cattle Show 1955
Glazed oil emulsion
60.9 x 98.7 cm
Private Collection
Catalogue Raisonné No. 48

Cyclist and Crow 1981
Acrylic polymer emulsion
70.6 x 100.0 cm
Collection Lavalin Inc.
Catalogue Raisonné No. 119

Sign and Harrier 1970
Acrylic polymer emulsion
83.6 cm diameter
Musée national d'art moderne–Centre
    Georges Pompidou
Catalogue Raisonné No. 82

The reference to "a story never to be told" and the darkness and chill of dread that hangs over the picture brings up the political undertones in Colville's later work. Colville has referred to the tensions of the times in which we live as expressed in a poem by W.B. Yeats, "The Second Coming." Yeats' poem, published in 1921, is a reflection on spiritual aridity at a time of political and social upheaval in Ireland:

> Turning and turning in the widening gyre
> The falcon cannot hear the falconer;
> Things fall apart; the centre cannot hold;
> Mere anarchy is loosed upon the world,
> The blood-dimmed tide is loosed, and everywhere
> The ceremony of innocence is drowned;
> The best lack all conviction, while the worst
> Are full of passionate intensity.
>
> Surely some revelation is at hand;
> Surely the Second Coming is at hand.
> The Second Coming! Hardly are those words out
> When a vast image of *Spiritus Mundi*
> Troubles my sight: somewhere in the sands of the desert
> A shape with lion body and the head of a man,
> A gaze blank and pitiless as the sun,
> Is moving its slow thighs, while all about it
> Reel shadows of the indignant desert birds.
> The darkness drops again; but now I know
> That twenty centuries of stony sleep
> Were vexed to nightmare by a rocking cradle,
> And what rough beast, its hour come round at last,
> Slouches towards Bethlehem to be born?[20]

The poem is deeply pessimistic, the promise of the Second Coming is fraught with an anxiety that a new and destructive force will come to shatter the values of Christianity. Colville's picture, too, expresses the precariousness of civil values; "the centre cannot hold" when spiritual values are so uncertain; "what rough beast...Slouches towards Bethlehem ...?" as we follow the homing crows to their distant and dark wood destination?

By depicting animals Colville shows us an aspect of communication, an example of something united with its surroundings. By contrast they point to how we are frequently disoriented, uncertain, and anxious. So often, locked into our own worlds, we avoid contact with the world or grasp it through tenuous and indirect means. These aspects are the subjects of two closely related paintings of 1962, *Ocean Limited* and *Departure* (CR 65 and 66).

Crow Up Early 1966
Acrylic polymer emulsion
45.7 x 68.5 cm
Private Collection
Catalogue Raisonné No. 76

Ocean Limited 1962
Oil and synthetic resin
68.5 x 119.3 cm
Collection William A.M. Burden & Co.
Catalogue Raisonné No. 65

Seven Crows 1980
Acrylic polymer emulsion
60.0 x 120.0 cm
Ross B. Eddy
Catalogue Raisonné No. 118

Ravens at the Dump 1965
Serigraph, edition 19
30.5 x 68.6 cm
Catalogue Raisonné No. 130

Border Collie 1972
Serigraph, edition 500
11.4 x 11.4 cm
Catalogue Raisonné No. 136

Crow and Sheep 1976
Acrylic polymer emulsion
30.4 cm diameter
Private Collection, Vancouver
Catalogue Raisonné No. 108

Three Sheep 1954
Casein tempera
30.4 x 49.1 cm
Lincoln Kirstein
Catalogue Raisonné No. 45

Swimming Dog and Canoe 1979
Acrylic polymer emulsion
53.4 x 119.4 cm
Private Collection, Geneva
Catalogue Raisonné No. 115

Owl 1970
Acrylic polymer emulsion
22.8 x 30.4 cm
Kitchener-Waterloo Art Gallery, Ontario
Catalogue Raisonné No. 84

Crow with Silver Spoon 1972
Serigraph, edition 70
45.7 cm diameter
Catalogue Raisonné No. 135

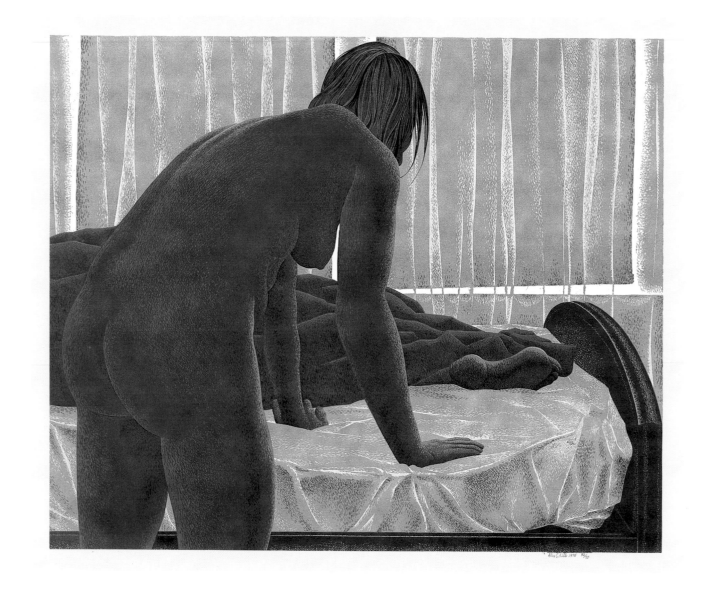

Sleeper 1975
Serigraph, edition 70
43.0 x 53.4 cm
Mira Godard Gallery
Catalogue Raisonné No. 137

Snow 1969
Serigraph, edition 70
61.0 x 45.7 cm
Mira Godard Gallery
Catalogue Raisonné No. 133

189

The man in *Ocean Limited* was not based on a member of his family nor a close friend but was someone Colville frequently saw. "Ocean Limited" is the express train that runs between Montreal and Halifax. The picture, based on strict parallels and opposed movements, sets up a conflict between the man and the locomotive, but one of indifference, not of collision. The parallel structure and the separation between the train and the man asserts the independence of the one and the efficiency of the other. They operate at different rates and levels of progress so that the meeting between them becomes irrelevant; neither the movement of the man or the train can be deflected by the other. But there is, as always, the element of the spectator. Here the standpoint of the viewer is drawn to the meeting point between man and train, which lies not in the centre of the picture but over to the left, marked by the telephone pole. It stands at the point of their meeting and marks the separation between them. For all its rushing convergence the painting is, in essence, a statement in non-communication. It is only the viewer, through the artist, who relates them.

In *Departure*, by contrast, the picture is not cast in parallels but on diagonals; the setting of the quay, the telephone kiosk, and the ship all follow the same angle. This flow brings a gentle but tenuous relationship between the elements, emphasizing their gradual separation. They are linked only by implication through the woman using the telephone. The implication, however, is strong precisely because it is convincing to the imagination. It is reminiscent of Wallace Stevens' linking the lasting conviction of the imagination with the real:

> The imagination loses vitality as it ceases to adhere to what is real. When it adheres to the unreal and intensifies what is unreal, while its first effect may be extraordinary, that effect is the maximum effect that it will ever have.[21]

The capacity of the imagination is drained by images dominated by distance from reality. That loss to the imagination occurs when we dismiss an image because of its unreality or seek to substantiate it with a fixed meaning. Then there is no imaginative image but only what Coleridge described as a work of fancy, a work in which there is no "movement," just a description of objects whose relationships are fixed and static. In *Departure* the reality of the image remains convincing to the imagination because the tension between the movement and communication is irresolvable.

There is one group of works, interestingly all serigraphs, in which the force of communication is made through subject matter of a close and intimate sort. These are works in which two figures are present on an equal basis, a man and a woman, nude or partly clothed. In many other works the man is placed in the situation of an observing figure,

Departure 1962
Oil and synthetic resin
45.7 x 66.0 cm
Kestner-Gesellschaft, Hanover, West
    Germany
Catalogue Raisonné No. 66

Hotel Maid 1978
Serigraph, edition 100
24.1 x 20.0 cm
Mira Godard Gallery
Catalogue Raisonné No. 140

or the two figures are turned away from each other, as in *June Noon* or *January* (CR 69 and 86). To these serigraphs, *After Swimming* (1955), *Snow* (1969), and *Sleeper* of 1975 (CR 123, 133 and 137), we should add *Woman with Brassiere* of 1958 (CR 126), for although it contains just one figure, it has the same intimacy of mood as the others. The settings are simple, details reduced to a minimum, and the emphasis on the close relationship between the figures draws us into that atmosphere of intimacy. The gestures, like the settings, are simple, the man wrapping a towel around the woman's shoulders, the woman putting on her brassiere or garter belt or leaning on a bed over a sleeping figure. Colville's choice of the serigraph technique adds to that quiet atmosphere. His painting technique, by the mid-1950s, tended toward firm and clear edges, and an even focus for each element. In contrast the technique he uses for the serigraphs is more open and the effect gives a softer atmospheric quality.

In these works the sense of communication is brought about through a subtle and gentle stating of events, bearing on the intimate elements of a relationship. Their expressive capacity is found in the warmth and gentleness of slight gestures and in an openness and familiarity that relies on mutual trust and respect. This mutuality speaks in a personal sense to the most important relationship in Colville's own life, that between himself and his wife. The works also respond to his belief that balance and security within one's personal life is essential for the ability to show open interpersonal expression. This means, for him, that a sense of security and trust is vital before it is possible to express with sincerity the closeness of a relationship.

For many artists, of course, the expression – indeed the expiation – of inner tumult has been the motivation to artistic expression. Painters like van Gogh and Jackson Pollock and writers like James Joyce and Samuel Beckett show the extraordinary power of genius to give concrete expression to all that is unsettled, confused, and difficult. For Colville the questions of life and of death, the existential question of being in the here and now, are essential for serious art. But rather than opening up the dreadful absurdity of life, he moves toward asserting the values in life on which the individual can depend. A relationship of love, a sense of trust and responsibility, are the values in which both his life and his work are grounded. His inalienable belief in the intrinsic strength of those values is what enables him to give objective form, through art, to all that is most personal to him in ways that are neither betrayal nor exploitation. This foundation underlies all his work, but it has special force in those images where he touches on the closest and strongest of personal relationships.

Woman with Brassiere 1958
Serigraph, edition 16
36.7 x 33.8 cm
Catalogue Raisonné No. 126

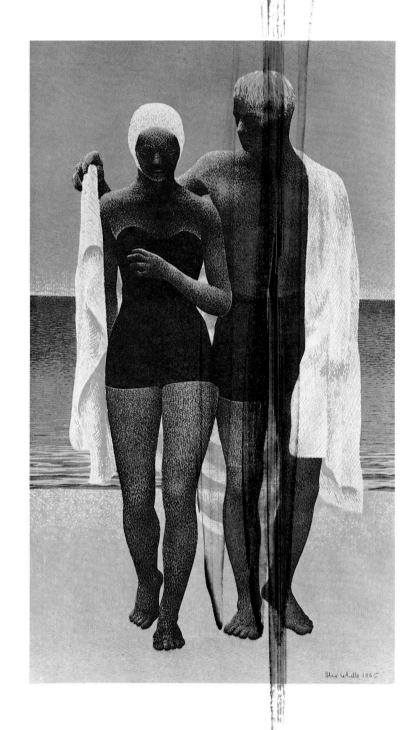

After Swimming 1955
Serigraph, edition 27
63.5 x 38.1 cm
Private Collection
Catalogue Raisonné No. 123

Sunrise 1970
Serigraph, edition 70
30.5 x 61.0 cm
Catalogue Raisonné No. 134

Harbour 1975
Acrylic polymer emulsion
33.0 x 53.3 cm
Private Collection
Catalogue Raisonné No. 105

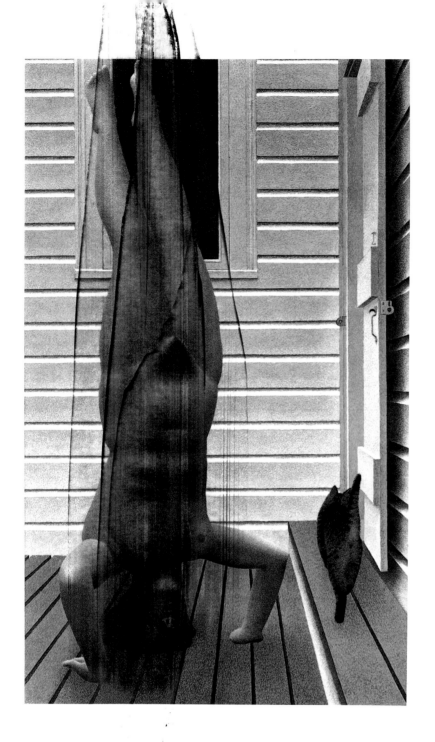

Headstand 1982
Acrylic polymer emulsion
66.0 x 40.8 cm
Fischer Fine Art, London
Catalogue Raisonné No. 121

SIX

THE NOTION OF GRACE: SELF AND FAMILY AS SUBJECT

It is a mark of special creative talent when, in reviewing the career of an artist, it is wrong to separate the work he has produced from the life he has led. For Colville's career this aspect has a special meaning, because the subjects he has chosen to paint refer directly and openly to the circumstances of his life. One way to respond to this subject matter is to see him as a regionalist artist, someone whose work draws exclusively from a limited locality, heightening our appreciation of it. Even rejecting the stigma of parochialism that is often, and wrongly, attached to regionalism, it is simply misconstruing Colville's work to see it in these terms. The regionalist view is the dominant historical approach to art in Canada, and a substantial one for contemporary art.

Colville's work has often been seen as part of a Maritimes Realist school of which he is the "father." There is no question that his work and his teaching has had a substantial effect on many artists in the Maritimes; Hugh MacKenzie, Mary Pratt, Tom Forrestall, and D.P. Brown were students of his at Mount Allison, and Christopher Pratt attended the university while Colville was on staff. To press the connections too far, however, is to do a disservice to all the artists, for two reasons. First because such an approach rests on simplified assumptions about regionalism; and second because it overlooks the failure of criticism to establish clear distinctions between different approaches to realist painting.

Considerable attention has been shown in Germany to Colville's work. Between 1963 and 1976 eleven of his pictures, a substantial proportion of his production, were acquired by private collectors in Germany. And it was German critic Heinz Ohff who wrote that Colville may be, "the most prominent, indeed the most important realist painter in the Western world."[1] Ohff approached the question of regionalism in an interesting way by titling his article "As provincial as Caspar David Friedrich," picking up on Colville's statement that "I am a provincial artist." In these terms, "provincial" does not mean "blinkered," but rather reflects a sensitivity to the limitations by which all of us are bound. The sense in which Colville uses "provincial" is an assertion of individuality. His disinterest in other movements of art arises not from a perverse desire to assert his difference but from the conviction of his particular needs and vision.

The German interest in his work from the 1960s parallels the interest in the United States in the early 1950s. Colville's first dealer was in New York and a number of his paintings were bought by American collectors. The sources of Colville's early work are, as we have seen, to be found substantially in American painting, in his admiration of Thomas Eakins, Edward Hopper, Ben Shahn and, in general, of American figurative painting of the late 1930s and early 1940s. This was the context from which his work was developed and

fig. 24
Study for River Thames November 16, 1972
Ink
27.2 x 35.4 cm
Collection the artist

fig. 25
Study for River Thames November 16, 1972
Ink
27.2 x 35.4 cm
Collection the artist

was recognized as such in New York. German painting, over many centuries, has carried a vein of strong and stark realism which has continued into our century, enjoying a powerful surge of interest among young painters in recent years. Colville's paintings, seen outside of their localized context, has clearly struck chords in those brought up with that tradition of German painting.

The integrity of Colville's work is measured by the fact that he chooses to express himself through subject matter immediately identifiable with his own circumstances. He does not strain after effects that lie outside his experience. His work is concerned with the great events in the lives of each one of us – of living and dying, of love, of communication – and he brings that to us through his own experience, through his family and the locality he knows best.

Several groups of works underline the relationship between the personal reflections on which Colville depends and the experience of us all. In particular these works concentrate on images in which he uses himself and members of his family. The person he most frequently uses for the female figures in his pictures is his wife; but his daughter Ann has also been the model for a number of pictures. She was the model for the young child in *Child and Dog* (CR 29) and six years later for the girl in *Child Skipping* (CR 57). Colville followed the process of her growing up in two other pictures, *August* (CR 73) made in 1964, and then ten years later in *The River Thames* (CR 104). These paintings do not form a portrait series, but he was sensitive both as a father and as an artist to the process of his children growing up and it is natural that he should express this through those close to him.

Each element in the pictures is finely adjusted in mood, and their settings are precisely chosen. In the first, *Child and Dog*, the setting is a confined domestic interior and *Child Skipping* marks the girl's emerging independence, suspended between home and school, play and work. *August* and *River Thames* are more subtle, as the girl recognizes the complexities in the world around her. Colville shows this not only in the greater range of elements within the pictures, but also through the brilliant descriptions of tone and colour and atmosphere. The two paintings respond to each other in a number of ways: the setting of the figures in relation to a bridge and houses; the contrast between the teenage girl in a rural town setting and the young woman in the city. The link with home and with the often awkward passing of childhood, shown in *August*, stands against adult independence in the anonymity of a great city in *River Thames* (figs. 24, 25). Colville underlines these contrasts by the viewpoints of the pictures. In *August* the low viewpoint seems to emphasize the sense of isolation and loneliness so characteristic of adolescent emotions. She is awkward and out of place, despite the fact that she is still rooted

Woman, Dog and Canoe 1982
Serigraph, edition 70
43.1 x 69.8 cm
Catalogue Raisonné No. 145

fig. 26
Wynn Chamberlain (American, 1929-)
Celebration 1954-55
Egg tempera on composition board
140.3 x 72.4 cm
Collection Whitney Museum of American
   Art, Gift of the Pastorale Fund

to her environment. In *River Thames*, on the other hand, the young woman is firmly enclosed by the circumstances of the life around her. Her feet are solidly placed on the ground, and the grey reality of the day encloses her. Here is the reality beyond the wish of dreams; the skipping-rope of *Child Skipping* is exchanged for an umbrella.

Centred around the process of one person growing up, the pictures show the developing complexity of an individual life, expanding to touch many facets of time. For the young child reality appears to exist only in a direct and physical way. The young adult in *River Thames* is held within the circumstances of which her individuality, her portion of time, is only one measure. The river and the buildings that line its banks are not dependent on this one woman's life, but her being there establishes one particular circumstance of time. Her life is inseparable from those surroundings, weaving her background into them. Each element has its own particular time frame; the flow of the river, the schedule of the bus, and the buildings, whose mixture of architecture reflects a long process of change. This setting recalls the opening lines of T.S. Eliot's "East Coker":

> In my beginning is my end. In succession
> Houses rise and fall, crumble, are extended,
> Are removed, destroyed, restored.... [2]

This interweaving of time and space marks also the way in which people fill their lives. Colville has said that the questions that had to be answered, particularly by North American artists, were "Who are we?"; "What are we like?"; "*What do we do?*" [my emphasis].[3] This is the question raised by the painting *Main Street* of 1979 (CR 114). The setting is precise and, for Colville, familiar. This is Main Street in Wolfville, the town where he has lived since 1973 and where, since he was a boy, he has regularly spent his summers. The yellow Renault is parked in front of the Wolfville postal station and the war memorial which was erected after World War I. For many years Colville had wanted to find a way of using the memorial in a picture; he had even made drawings of it in the 1950s. His fascination was, in part, stimulated by *Celebration*, a painting by the American artist Wynn Chamberlain made in 1954-55 (fig. 26) of which Edwin Hewitt had sent him a photograph. Chamberlain's picture, openly allegorical, shows couples dancing in a graveyard around a war memorial. In the middle ground is a town with churches, factories, and houses, and beyond that a landscape with rolling hills to one side and a steep cliff, cut away like a wound, to the other. The sky is a disturbing mixture of fair-weather cirro-cumulus and storm clouds. The picture is overflowing with metaphors of death and debt, unity and enjoyment, security and threat.

fig. 27
Photograph of the Wolfville Postal Station

Colville's sense of the potential in the Main Street was suddenly realized when he saw that the everyday business of shopping could form the occasion for it. His painting is not, as was Chamberlain's, an allegory but a statement of the present, set in authentic circumstances. In the course of working on the picture he made a number of subtle adjustments to the site – the memorial is given more prominence and details are clarified; he closes up the distance between the spectator's position and the houses at the back, as if we were looking through a telephoto lens (fig. 27). *Main Street* has, like *River Thames*, a complex interweaving of references to time, but here through a contrast of occupations. The statue, with its memory of the dead, is a reminder that war – no matter how distant in time – has a pervasive effect on the present. Against this reminder the women's preoccupation with shopping sets the reference to death and destruction against the preservation and continuity of life.

The strength of the picture lies in its naturalness. There is no straining after meaning, for every element has its rightful place and the significance of things exists in all we do and see. Reality lies in the totality of life's circumstances, its continuities and discontinuities, its constructions and destructions. There is, as Colville shows it, no such thing as a gratuitous act. And yet, as so often in his work, there is a sense in which no matter how commonplace events are, they cannot escape an element of uncertainty, a tension that we cannot quite name. Every part of this picture is even and sharp in focus with one exception, that of the shape formed by condensation in the window of

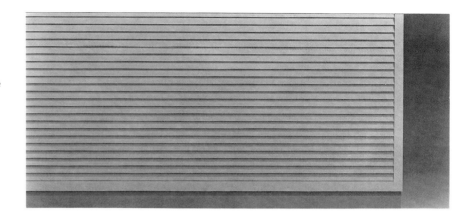

fig. 28
Christopher Pratt (Canadian, 1935-)
March Night 1976
Oil on masonite
101.4 x 228.6 cm
Collection Art Gallery of Ontario, Purchase
with assistance from Wintario, 1977

the car. It is like the shadow of someone sitting in the driver's seat. The viewing level of the picture, as so often, is low, and the spectator's position is related to this "ghost" image. Its position reflects our own, setting us between the women carrying the shopping bags and the memorial. For Colville this sense of a consciousness – or the spectator's identification of and with his consciousness within the picture – is absolutely crucial.

In many respects Colville's understanding of the position of the spectator is more significantly related to the devices of fiction than it is to painting. In reading a novel (and Colville, as I have said, is an avid reader of fiction) we must, in each case, come to terms with how, as a reader, we are placed in the text. Do we identify with one character? Are we a surrogate narrator of the text? Are we listening to someone telling the story to us? And how do we relate the views expressed in the text with what we understand to be the viewpoint of the author? Colville has spoken of this issue in regard to his reading of Joseph Conrad: "You are listening to a person tell you of his experience in Conrad...it is a way of drawing the person in."[4] And he contrasts his approach to that of Christopher Pratt (fig. 28),

> I once said to Christopher Pratt that the real difference between our stuff is that...the person in his paintings or prints is the person who is looking at them, the consciousness is outside the work. For me this is absolutely out. There has to be an [internal] consciousness, who could be animal or human.[5]

In addition there is Colville's use of the low viewpoint, as if seen from a car seat. In part such a viewpoint gives a sense of relief and monumentality to the figures so that they dominate their surroundings. But more than that, the car-seat level relates to a particular and modern view of the world, a view of our movement through events.

The geometry of Colville's paintings orients everything to their viewpoints, which are often based on the inclusion and effacement of himself in the pictures. He is so often in the pictures, but covers the identification by referring to himself (fictionally) as "the man in the picture," and frequently by having his features covered or by turning his back to us. This technique is an extension of the relationship of viewpoint and consciousness, and makes us aware of our position. Not only must we ask, "Who made this picture?", "Who is this person we see?" but also "Who, as we look, are we?"

This sense of questioning the place and identification of ourselves and of the artist means that we must come to terms both with our views and with what we understand of his. We must, for instance, reconcile Colville's statement that his work is fundamentally optimistic with the feeling of discomfort or of suspended threat that many of his paintings have. Colville has said that he believes in the notion of "grace," by which he means that there are *moments* when everything appears to be all right, that things are in their place and that one is insulated against fears and pressures. But if there are such moments it must mean that, at other times, the structure of our lives, materially, emotionally, or psychologically, is at risk. This awful tenuousness of our existence is what Colville believes we must come to terms with in order to structure our lives and relationships and expressions in a way that gives value to our existence. When Colville speaks of optimism he means that we must actively accept that responsibility.

Acceptance also means facing threat and tension, as we must in the painting *In the Woods* of 1976 (CR 109). In one way the subject is straightforward. Colville, who has long had an interest in firearms, joined a local gun club in 1974 for target shooting; the mask worn by the man is simply a precaution against the weather. But the origin of the picture is more specific and disturbing. Colville had been deeply impressed by a Bertolucci film, *The Conformist*, based on Alberto Moravia's novel, which he had read many years before. He was impressed by a "hair-raising scene" of a shooting in the woods at the end of the film. The painting reflects a latent violence, a faceless violence suspended over the action. The hammer of the pistol is cocked and the man holds the option of choice; he can continue to suspend the action or precipitate it by compressing the trigger. Unlike *Main Street*, which balances death and the continuity of life, *In the Woods* describes the raw aspect of threat, holding the potential for destruction whose aim and timing we cannot predict.

This presence of threat is also contained in *Target Pistol and Man* (CR 117) with its precisely rendered pistol, inactive but prepared for immediate use. It is a similar suspension to that of an earlier painting, *Pacific* (CR 78) of 1967. The making of this picture was directly related to the time Colville spent at the University of California at Santa Cruz. He and Rhoda arrived there in September, and the following month he began work on the painting, completing it about three months later. It is, with *River Spree*, the only picture since the war that he has made outside his own studio. The decision to accept the appointment (as, later, also with the invitation to Berlin) had not been an easy one for Colville. He had been deeply shocked by the death of President Kennedy in 1963 and was sensitive to how the optimism of Kennedy's presidency had so quickly dissolved, to be replaced by the agony of the United States' involvement in the Vietnam War. In 1967 the deep splits within that country were becoming apparent, and the painting responds to Colville's sense of the pent-up violence and instability within the structure of the society.

The painting points both to the present and the past. The man stands looking out at the Pacific Ocean; between him and the spectator is the table with the gun on it. The table, with a yardstick set directly into its surface, was his mother's working table. The gun is a Browning 1935, which was the type of weapon Colville had been issued during the war. All of these elements bear on the situation he found himself in – feelings of social and political tension, and the compressed potential for violence that easy access to firearms signified. In response to questions on this painting he has denied any connotations of suicide, but spoke of its having to do with murder.[6] He did not mean that the man in the picture was contemplating an act of violence, but rather that he is aware of the irony of the powers between which he is set. Behind him is the implication of violence and the expression of power through force of arms; in front of him the sea represents nature's power of continuity and its indifference to human events – signified in the meaning of "Pacific" both as the name of the ocean and literally "peaceful." The artist, as an observer and participant in society, has as much to do with pointing up what is evil as with showing what is good. Colville has said:

> …the subject matter is about the dichotomy in human life in which you think of things like purity and eternity…and peace and, if you like, God, or something like that…and the other side [is the] nasty business of actual life.[7]

This recalls a statement by the novelist and critic John Updike (a writer whom Colville admires), who has said the writer invariably has an affinity to his villain as well as his hero.[8] The circumstances which led him to paint *Pacific* had a coincidental but disturbing aftermath. Shortly after Colville finished the painting two further acts of political murder rocked the United States: the assassinations of Martin Luther King in March 1968 and of Robert Kennedy in June.

Sensitive both to good and evil, Colville believes that we have a responsibility to create stability, to build order through work. For him to express this responsibility means accepting a certain personal vulnerability because he can speak only from himself,

> What I am thinking is what *I* am thinking, not someone else. The only lives I know are my life, my wife's life...I don't know...your life and that's why I haven't painted you.[9]

His self-effacement in *Pacific* – the figure is modelled on himself – in part avoids an identification with personality because, although it derives from his experience, it is presented to the subjectivities of his viewers. In recent years, however, he has faced that issue of vulnerability more directly. "I thought," he has said, " 'Why should I always be hiding?' "[10]

This change is obvious in *Target Pistol and Man* (CR 117), as it was the year before in the painting *Refrigerator* (CR 111). This picture caused some criticism because of its frankness, but more important than its challenge to prudishness was its bold self-confrontation. The realist painter, unlike an abstractionist, can be compelled to overt self-revelation, literally self-exposure. Because he must confront the potential of threat that is always present, he brings that confrontation directly on himself, even if it means declaring his vulnerability. In his early works Colville approached these issues abstractly by giving his pictures generalized settings. But from the late 1950s, accepting that he had to work with images of direct realism, his work has become increasingly open.

This openness is manifested in many ways; in acceptance, in self-examination, and in dependence. We are all dependent on the circumstances of our lives and the relationships we build to the world. This notion of dependence is nowhere more critically shown than in Colville's treatment of blindness. It is a subject that he has been concerned with for more than a dozen years, first appearing in a drawing of 1968, *Seeing-Eye Dog and Man* (fig. 29) which in turn led to two paintings, *Dog and Bridge* in 1976 (CR 107) and *Night Walk* (CR 120) in 1981.

The setting of *Dog and Bridge* and the preceding drawings is on or near the railway bridge at Horton Landing that carries the track between Middleton and Windsor, Nova Scotia. The first idea in 1968, done in Santa Cruz where there was a similar bridge over a river (fig. 29), shows the dog and blind man walking on a path beside the Gaspereau River, east of Wolfville. The man is drawn as a shadowy figure, in contrast to the dog, whose attention is directed to the

fig. 29
Study for Seeing-Eye Dog and Man
    February 10-12, 1968
Pencil
18.4 x 27.9 cm
Collection the artist

spectator. When Colville returned to the idea at the end of 1975 (fig. 30), the setting is changed to the bridge and is retained in the painting *Dog and Bridge*, but the man is eliminated. The thrust of the picture is changed. In the drawings the composition expressed the interdependence between the man and the dog. In the painting, we are left uncertain of the dog's attitude. Is it hostile or friendly? The ambiguity in the picture is thrust onto us but is irresolvable, for we cannot penetrate the perceptions and instincts of the dog. But the structure of the picture allows us no escape. Even as we try to disperse our attention to the superstructure of the bridge etched against the sky, or to the rail lines curling away out of our vision, every element of the picture draws us back to face the steady gaze of the dog and our uncertainty.

Five years later Colville returned to the original idea of the blind man and the dog. For all its apparent simplicity and its small size, he made nearly thirty drawings for *Night Walk*. These describe the composition's geometry and the special demands of the night setting; a number of them are on black paper, to work on the complex tonal and colouristic balances. Further preparation for the painting took the form of SX70 photographs of himself as the man, to fix the pose and work out the proportional relationships. As so often, the final choice of viewpoint is consistent with someone passing in a car.

The picture is disturbing both in mood and subject matter. The darkness, cut only by the artificial brilliance of the street light, casts the foliage into a livid green. We know, of course, that the appearance of the setting is a matter of indifference to the man. His world of

Dog and Bridge 1976
Acrylic polymer emulsion
86.3 x 86.3 cm
Mr. & Mrs. J.H. Clark
Catalogue Raisonné No. 107

fig. 30
Study for Dog and Bridge
December 3-4, 1975
Pencil, ink and wash
27.2 x 31.3 cm
Collection the artist

darkness and the world of the dog, equally unknown to us, meet in their mutual dependence. Related by guidance and care and affection, they form a single unit moving equally from darkness to light and then again to darkness. It is an image taut with irony, for it portrays a subject that the subject can never know – a point underlined by the fact that the man is based on the memory of Colville's mother's father, who had died many years before. It is as if to say that we come from darkness and return to darkness. Furthermore, the picture is made by someone who is wholly dependent on his sight. For a painter to emphasize the fact of his eyesight is to walk on the edge of his own dependency, recognizing by what slight and frail means he is supported.

Night Walk is a particularly striking assertion of the artist's sense of dependence. But he expresses dependence in other ways, for instance, in regard to belonging. In a number of the early pictures, like *Woman, Jockey and Horse* and *Couple on Beach* (CR 31 and 55), the sense of the dependence is of the man on the woman. We have also seen a group of serigraphs in which the relationship between a man and a woman is presented in a spirit of equality.

In *June Noon* and *January* (CR 69 and 86), two pictures made eight years apart, the relationship between the two figures is very similar, carrying almost a musical relationship in their links and

Night Walk 1981
Acrylic polymer emulsion
45.7 x 45.7 cm
Fischer Fine Art, London
Catalogue Raisonné No. 120

The River Thames 1974
Acrylic polymer emulsion
76.2 x 76.2 cm
Mr. & Mrs. J.H. Clark
Catalogue Raisonné No. 104

Main Street 1979
Acrylic polymer emulsion
61.0 x 86.2 cm
Consolidated-Bathurst Inc.
Catalogue Raisonné No. 114

fig. 31
Study for Morning April 4, 1970
Ink and wash on grey paper
25.1 x 16.3 cm
Collection the artist

contrasts, their common forms and their inversions. In these two paintings, in which the figures are based on Colville and his wife, there is the distinction of the seasons, placed on opposite sides of the calendar. The positioning of the figures and the distance between them remains similar in both pictures, although the figures are reversed. The man, who faces us in *January*, exchanges his binoculars for sun-glasses in *June Noon*. The pose of the woman remains constant, although she is nude in the one and clothed in the other. The horizon of the sea is exchanged for a snow-covered landscape, and the enclosure of the tent changed to the rounded hillside. In both cases the images point to the separation of the figures being only temporary. In *June Noon* our line of sight from one figure to the other passes through the opening in the net flap, as though the man had only recently gone outside. In *January*, snowshoe tracks show that the two people had been standing together; the woman has paused to look back, the man has moved on. This turning away, marking different directions of attention, indicates not an indifference between them but a recognition of their individualities. Colville strongly believes that the strength of a relationship lies in the recognition of each person's independence. In these pictures dependence is based on independence, set into the rhythm of the continuity of the seasons. Relationships may change, but relationship does not; the seasons change but the pattern of their sequence is constant. The figures are equally balanced; if our attention is caught by one it does not deny the other. It is not the same as the equality in *Snow* (CR 133) – the harmony of a moment of shared intimacy – but the harmony of individuality.

Ten years after making *January* he returned to the same theme, again based on himself and his wife, in the serigraph *Morning* (CR 144). The links between *Morning* and the two earlier paintings are clear indications that, as far as the content of an image is concerned, he makes no essential distinction between serigraphs and paintings. *Morning* repeats the separation of the figures, the man to the left, the woman to the right. And as in *January*, where the figures were linked by the snowshoe prints, and in *June Noon* by the opening in the tent, so in *Morning* they are linked by the bed on which they sit.

Colville's idea for the two figures sitting on a bed, the man shaving and the woman looking in a mirror, first occurred in a drawing done in April, 1970 (fig. 31). Made just before working on *January*, it counters the coldness and openness of that painting with an image of warmth and intimacy. But after making a few drawings he abandoned the idea for the time being. Three years later he returned to it. In these 1973 drawings, similar to the final composition, the man sits on the far side of the bed facing away from us and the woman reclines, holding a

Snowstorm 1971
Acrylic polymer emulsion
22.8 x 30.4 cm
Private Collection
Catalogue Raisonné No. 85

January 1971
Acrylic polymer emulsion
60.9 x 81.2 cm
Collection of Toronto Dominion Bank,
  Toronto
Catalogue Raisonné No. 86

June Noon 1963
Acrylic polymer emulsion
76.2 x 76.2 cm
Private Collection, Düsseldorf, West
   Germany
Catalogue Raisonné No. 69

fig. 32
Study for Morning September 30, 1980
Ink and wash on board
13.8 x 22.5 cm
Collection the artist

fig. 33
Study for Morning August 24, 1970
Ink and washes on blue paper
30.3 x 22.8 cm
Collection the artist

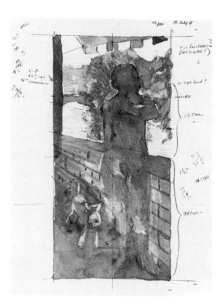

fig. 34
Study for River Spree July 15, 1971
Ink, wash and crayon
31.9 x 23.9 cm
Collection the artist

mirror in front of her face. Seven years passed before he again returned to the subject; first in sketches made in September 1980 (fig. 32) and then, after a further pause, in February 1981, when he settled on the precise form of the composition and made the print.

In some respects this picture has been one of his most obsessive images. The earlier drawings led not only to *Morning* but also to the 1973 painting *Woman in Bathtub* (CR 89) and to the 1971 painting *River Spree* (CR 87). The image of a woman holding a mirror in front of her face occurs in a drawing of 1970 (fig. 33). It is also found in drawings that Colville made when he and Rhoda were in Berlin in 1971 (fig. 34) and led, that year, to *River Spree*. And there is a further twist to this involved image. The mirror the woman holds in *Morning* is specifically identifiable; on a visit to the National Gallery in Berlin during 1971 Colville sketched an Egyptian bronze mirror he saw there, an artifact from the Eighteenth Dynasty (fig. 35a and 35b). The Egyptian word for a mirror is *ankh*, which also carries the meaning "life." This conjunction of meaning comes closer to the place the mirror has in *Morning* than the more traditional iconography in Western art, where the mirror is a symbol of "vanitas" or vanity.

The idea of the woman holding the mirror intrigued Colville because it allowed him to conceal the woman's face (avoiding personality) but to imply her self-identification. That device of literal and metaphoric self-reflection is echoed in the man, but in a different way. He faces away from us, toward a picture on the wall in front of him. This picture is one of Colville's early serigraphs *Cat on Fence* (CR 124). *Morning*, by having the figures nude, is literally revealing but metaphorically closed in on itself. The relationship between the two

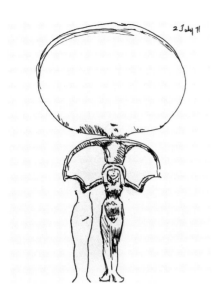

fig. 35a
Sketch of Egyptian Mirror July 2, 1971
Ink
18.2 x 13.0 cm
Collection the artist

fig. 35b
Egyptian Bronze Mirror
Eighteenth Dynasty
Ägyptisches Museum, Staatliche Museen,
    Berlin

figures is confined in the self-reflections in the mirror and the picture on the wall. The work speaks eloquently to their separateness in facing away from each other, combined with their closeness in reflection.

Morning is related to *June Noon* and *January* and also, by the woman holding a mirror, to *Woman in Bathtub* (CR 89). This image was first developed with just the figure of the woman (fig. 36), but the figure of the robed man behind her was soon introduced. The image is, for the spectator, both surprising and uncomfortable. The pose of the woman, the towering figure of the man, arbitrarily cut off at the level of his chest, and the contrast of the bodies against the hard white tiles and tub, all make it unsettling. Yet the scene is domestic and commonplace and refers to the long tradition of the bathing woman theme; Diana disturbed by Anteus, Venus at her toilet, Bathsheba spied on by David, Suzanna and the Elders. In the nineteenth century both Degas and Bonnard painted the subject; Colville has said his painting was influenced by Bonnard. But Bonnard's paintings are invested with an atmosphere of brilliant colour. In Colville's picture everything is cool, from the white bath tiles and the blue dressing gown to the colour of the woman's skin. It is hygienic rather than romantic, prosaic rather than poetic. The voyeurism of keyhole-peeping is denied; we are there, in the room.

Yet the painting has its place within Colville's subjects. We have seen many with just the two figures, male and female, and in them he describes the scenes with directness to the facts of a relationship. If we feel a sense of threat in the picture it lies in our presence at the scene. For it is only in the spectator that the polarities of discomfort and domesticity exist. Why? Because even in the simple acts of everyday living we are not free of our anxieties, the fear of warmth leading to cool, of vitality leading to its negation. And because the painter works primarily through the creation of space, it is above all in his presentation of space that the picture is unsettling; in particular the arbitrary slicing of the figures and the way that the bathtub is opened towards us. It is only from our viewpoint that the figures are cut, which makes us intruders into the scene.

In the way that *January* drew its elements from *June Noon*, so *Woman in Bathtub* reflects a theme that Colville had used in his 1965 painting *To Prince Edward Island* (CR 74). This picture, as so many others, was the result of long consideration. The first idea for the subject came in a pen sketch of 1960 (fig. 37), in which the woman holds the binoculars and the man next to her turns away. Three years later he made a drawing with the man holding the binoculars, and again in a sketch of 1965 (fig. 38). But immediately after this date he establishes the arrangement with the woman holding the binoculars and the man behind her (fig. 39). The drawings that followed were

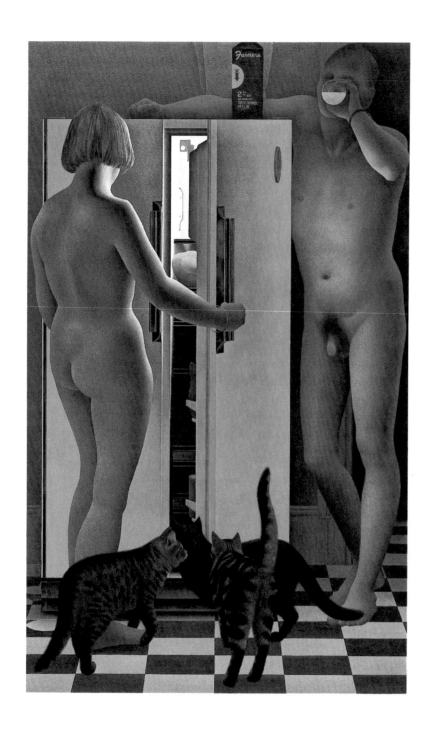

Refrigerator 1977
Acrylic polymer emulsion
120.0 x 74.0 cm
Private Collection
Catalogue Raisonné No. 111

Morning 1981
Serigraph, edition 70
54.6 cm diameter
Mira Godard Gallery
Catalogue Raisonné No. 144

fig. 36
Study for Woman in Bathtub
March 7-9, 1973
Pencil, inks and crayon
30.5 x 42.4 cm
Collection the artist

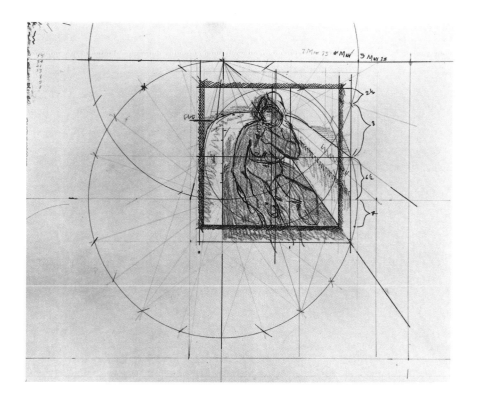

concerned with the authentication process, fixing the positions of the figures and making precise drawings of them and of the life boat and davits. As with *Main Street* he had an image in mind from 1960, but he could not find the circumstances to realize it;

> I was intrigued with the idea of two people, one looking through binoculars, and I had tried out little sketchy versions for some time, but I had never found anything that seemed quite adequate. So I discarded the idea. Why was I intrigued? I don't know; just that there was *something* I sensed in it. It had some *meaning*. After a trip to Prince Edward Island in 1965 I suddenly realized that I was going to be able to work the two people and the binoculars – that the boat would do it –."[11]

The painting was a major achievement. In its simple, striking composition and its remarkable clarity it was a turning point in his art, gathering many aspects that he had developed in the mid-1950s and projecting them into the work he subsequently made. It marks the self-effacement of the man and the far-sighted vision of the woman. Although they both look in the same direction he can see only as far as her. The setting on the boat insulates them from other events; for the duration of the voyage they reflect on their own visions. He is the observer, watching the woman and responding to her through the

fig. 37
Study for To Prince Edward Island
   February 4, 1960
Ink
27.0 x 37.2 cm
Collection the artist

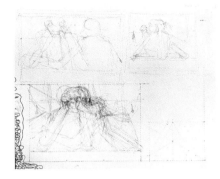

fig. 38
Study for To Prince Edward Island
   June 17, 1965
Pencil and ink
27.2 x 34.7 cm
Collection the artist

brilliant precision of his work. But of her vision he can say nothing; he can be specific only about what he sees. To say that the picture was a turning point means, above all, that it seals his identification as an observer. He cannot escape that anymore than he can escape himself, or the two figures in the painting can escape the conveyance of the boat. He is held wholly within his vision; he cannot *know* anyone else's vision, he can only project it.

Many people have written and spoken of an underlying sense of menace and threat in Colville's paintings. Harry Bruce describing *Couple on Beach* (CR 55) wrote, "Can she be dead? No, of course not, but what is it? What's *wrong*?[12] What's wrong, it seems to me, is that the images strike directly at the means by which we describe our world. Our understanding of the world and all the events it contains are expressed in terms of space and time. Our picture of the world, shifting at every moment, comprises our sensory perceptions and the contents of our minds in a complex of the immediate and the past. That the picture remains relatively stable reflects our ability to shift and balance, within fractions of seconds, that extraordinary mass of perceptions, notions, judgements, and prejudices.

Colville's paintings, with their cool surfaces, their mathematical rigour, and their evenly cast focus, cut into that mass with razor sharpness. And in doing that they present us with a view that is almost

Woman in Bathtub 1973
Acrylic polymer emulsion
86.3 x 86.3 cm
Collection Art Gallery of Ontario, Purchase
  with assistance from Wintario, 1978
Catalogue Raisonné No. 89

To Prince Edward Island 1965
Acrylic polymer emulsion
60.9 x 91.4 cm
National Gallery of Canada, Ottawa
Catalogue Raisonné No. 74

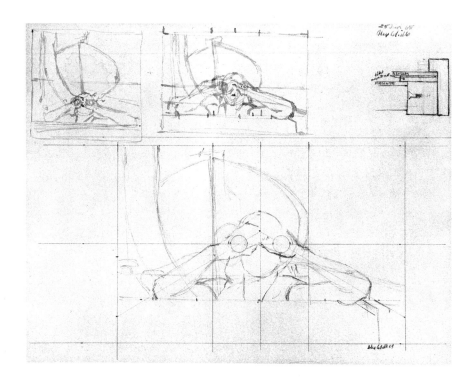

fig. 39
Study for To Prince Edward Island
June 25, 1965
Pencil and ink
27.9 x 35.6 cm
Dr. Helen J. Dow

all space and no time. We can describe the space in every picture down to the finest detail, we can discuss a rational order that sets the intervals between one object and another. But we cannot grasp the same certainty with respect to time. How do we deal with images that are simultaneously timeless and comprised of the most fleeting of moments? How do we cope with a world whose measure of space is open to the finest investigation but whose sense of time defies the terms we bring to comprehend it? This is the real threat for which there is no solution. We cannot treat the images as if they were photographs, for the conventions of space in photographs are related to an exact moment in time – this particular extension of space as it existed for that one hundredth of a second. The momentary state that a photograph records is selected out of time; we can reconstruct the moments before and the moments after. In a painting by Colville we cannot construct such a narrative that will satisfy the actual fact of the painting. We can, at best, repeat Bertrand Russell's description of Joseph Conrad's philosophy. Russell said that Conrad considered,

> civilized and morally tolerable human life as a dangerous walk on a thin crust of barely cooled lava, which at any moment might break and let the unwary sink into fiery depths.[13]

Colville's work acutely expresses this relativity in existence. But just as he is aware of our instability in the world and of the potential for evil, so also is he aware of the presence of good. He finds this in the example of the animal world, in the stabilizing responsibility of work, and in the power and the value of love.

In the final result it is good that predominates: his family, his attachment to the Maritimes, and his work. These are the core of his life. To the outside world it is in his work that his essence lies, in the meticulous standards of quality and seriousness of content of his paintings. Subjective and restricted in his choice of subjects and locales, his determined honesty reaches into the experience of a wide and varied audience. Concerned with issues that are absolutely fundamental to the life of the individual, Colville has deliberately chosen to work outside the questions that have dominated painting in this century. His interests lie in questions that are timeless and yet rooted in time; the course of a man's life as it is interwoven with the public and private demands made on him. His work expresses values that heighten our realization of what it means to be an individual, not by theoretical speculation but by the direct, day-by-day engagement with the world.

Pacific 1967
Acrylic polymer emulsion
53.3 x 53.3 cm
Private Collection, Toronto
Catalogue Raisonné No. 78

In the Woods 1976
Acrylic polymer emulsion
34.2 x 59.3 cm
Private Collection, Montreal
Catalogue Raisonné No. 109

May Day 1970
Acrylic polymer emulsion
43.1 x 43.1 cm
Collection of the Lynnwood Arts Centre,
    Simcoe, Ontario
Catalogue Raisonné No. 83

Summer in Town 1973
Acrylic polymer emulsion
30.4 x 45.7 cm
Mr. & Mrs. Donald MacKenzie
Catalogue Raisonné No. 90

Looking Up 1975
Acrylic polymer emulsion
30.4 x 26.3 cm
Private Collection
Catalogue Raisonné No. 106

Woman Carrying Canoe 1972
Acrylic polymer emulsion
48.2 x 83.8 cm
Private Collection
Catalogue Raisonné No. 88

Laser 1976
Acrylic polymer emulsion
57.7 x 100.0 cm
Staatliche Museen zu Berlin, DDR
Catalogue Raisonné No. 110

At Grand Pré 1982
Acrylic polymer emulsion
68.0 x 96.0 cm
Fischer Fine Art, London
Catalogue Raisonné No. 122

New Moon 1980
Serigraph, edition 70
36.0 x 45.0 cm
Catalogue Raisonné No. 143

ONE: THE ART OF ALEX COLVILLE

1 "Some thoughts about my painting," unpublished statement, November 29, 1973.

2 "Alex Colville, Wolfeville [sic], Nova Scotia," *Statements–18 Canadian Artists* (Regina: Norman Mackenzie Art Gallery, 1967), p. 36.

3 Robert E. Wood, *Martin Buber's Ontology: An Analysis of I and Thou* (Evanston, Ill.: Northwestern University Press, 1969), p. 5.

4 "An Artist in Canada," Brockington Lecture, Queen's University, Kingston, Ont., November 16, 1981.

5 See note 1.

6 In "Notes for Marina Vaizey," July 28, 1976. Unpublished, but see *Alex Colville: Paintings and Drawings (1970-1977)*, Kunsthalle, Düsseldorf and Fischer Fine Art, London, 1977.

7 He used oil emulsion in CR 52 and 53 and oil paint in resin gel in CR 57-66 and 68.

8 This excludes the lost *Self-Portrait* of 1942, see CR 154.

9 See note 6.

10 Silverpoint is a technique of drawing on a gesso-prepared paper or board with a piece of silver wire.

11 See note 2.

12 See Helen Gardner, *The Composition of Four Quartets* (London: Faber and Faber, 1978), p. v.

13 John Dewey, *Art as Experience* (New York: Capricorn Books, G.P. Putnam's Sons, 1958), p. 56.

TWO: THE EARLY YEARS: THE ARTIST AT THE THRESHOLD

1 "Alex Colville on Alex Colville," *Alex Colville: Diary of a War Artist*, compiled by Graham Metson and Cheryl Lean (Halifax: Nimbus Publishing, 1981), p. 21.

2 "An Artist in Canada," Brockington Lecture, 1981.

3 See Hugh Halliday, "Introduction" in *Alex Colville: Diary of a War Artist*, pp. 10-14.

4 Interview with artist July 27, 1982. References are to a series of interviews by the author with the artist held on July 27, 28, and 29, 1982.

5 Letter from H.O. McCurry to Charles Comfort, January 7, 1943 in National Gallery of Canada files.

6 See *Alex Colville: Diary of a War Artist*.

7 *Ibid*.

8 *Ibid*, pp. 59, 18.

9 *Ibid*, p. 123.

10 *Ibid*, p. 150.

11 *Ibid*, p. 92.

12 Interview with artist July 28, 1982.

13 "My experience as a Painter and Some General Views of Art." In Dow, pp. 203-208.

14 Dow, p. 204.

15 *Ibid*.

16 The Mexican painters had a major influence on American artists associated with the WPA/FPA programs.

17 Walter Abell, "Canadian Aspirations in Painting," *Culture* 3 (1942): 181.

18 Dow, p. 206.

19 C.G. Jung, "On the Relation of Analytical Psychology to Poetry," *The Spirit in Man, Art, and Literature* in *The Portable Jung*, edited by Joseph Campbell, (Harmondsworth: Penguin Books, 1976), p. 321.

20 Henry Moore was also one of Harry Fischer's "discoveries"; he has enjoyed a long-standing relationship with the Fischer gallery.

21 Miller Brittain (1912-1968). His early style followed that of the American Social Realists, but after the war he turned to a private form of Surrealism.

22 Edmond Jabès (1912–), *At the Threshold of the Book: The Book of Questions*, translated by Rosemarie Waldrop, (Middletown, Conn.: Wesleyan University Press, 1972), p. 17.

23 Interview with artist July 28, 1982.

THREE: THE MID-FIFTIES: ART AS AUTHENTICATION

1 Colville has made twenty-two serigraphs between 1955 and 1982. See CR 122-140, 142-145. He also made a set of lithographs on *Labours of the Months*, CR 141, based on a set of twelve paintings made in 1974, CR 92-103.

2 Letter from Alex Colville to D. Buchanan, March 4, 1958 in files of the National Gallery of Canada.

3 In conversation July 28, 1982.

4 Wallace Stevens, "The Relations between Poetry and Painting," *The Necessary Angel* (New York: Vintage Books, 1951), p. 164.

5 Dow, p. 72.

6 Roy Campbell, *Collected Poems I* (London: Bodley Head, 1949), p. 177.

7 Dow, p. 41.

8 Roy Campbell, *Light on a Dark Horse: An Autobiography 1901-1935* (London: Hollis and Carter, 1951).

9 In conversation July 27, 1982.

10 Epicurus (c. 341–c. 270 BC), a Greek philosopher and founder of the *Epicurean School*.

11   In conversation July 29, 1982.

12   Dow, p. 69.

13   Alfred H. Barr, Jr., *Painting and Sculpture in The Museum of Modern Art* (New York: The Museum of Modern Art, 1942).

14   *Symbolic Realists* (New York: Hewitt Gallery, 1950), n.p.

15   The Works Progress Administration/Federal Art Project (WPA/FAP) was established in 1935, a development from three existing New Deal projects to aid artists during the Depression. The first, the Public Works of Art Project, was initiated in December 1933. Under the programs artists were given commissions for murals in public buildings, as well as support for production of smaller works. The WPA/FAP was closed in April 1943, but the programs had a major, even a decisive, effect on the strength of the visual arts in the United States after the war.

16   See *George Tooker: Paintings 1947-1973*, (San Francisco: The Fine Arts Museums of San Francisco, 1974). In particular catalogue nos. 1-8.

FOUR: FALLING INTO WATER: FOCUSSING ON BALANCE AND CONTROL

1   Interview with artist July 29, 1982.

2   Interview with artist July 27, 1982.

3   Interview with artist July 28, 1982.

4   Interview with artist July 28, 1982.

5   "Notes for Marina Vaizey," July 28, 1976. Unpublished.

6   Richard Cork, "70 Years Ferment–But it Leaves This Painter Cold," *Evening Standard* (London) 20 January 1970.

7   Patrick A.E. Hutchings, "Realism, Surrealism and Celebration: The Paintings of Alex Colville in the Collection of the National Gallery of Canada," *Bulletin* no. 8 (1966), Ottawa: National Gallery of Canada, p. 19.

8   Interview with artist July 28, 1982.

9   *Statements –18 Canadian Artists*, pp. 35-36.

FIVE: THE ARTIST AS A RESPONSIBLE MAN

1   Interview with artist July 27, 1982.

2   Interview with artist July 28, 1982.

3   Interview with artist July 28, 1982.

4   T.S. Eliot, "The Dry Salvages," *Four Quartets*, 1979 (1944), London: Faber and Faber, pp. 33-34.

5   On a drawing for *Snowplow* Colville inscribed "envy of man who does not do anything. Bonjour M. Colville. Courbet–political and erotic."

6   Dow, p. 113.

7   *Ibid.*

8   See Dow, p. 207.

9   Robert Melville, "Alex Colville," London, Marlborough Fine Art (London) Ltd., January-February 1970, p. 8.

10   Interview with artist July 27, 1982.

11   Interview with artist July 28, 1982.

12   Interview with artist July 28, 1982.

13   See Klee's notes PN 26 M/S 45 p54a (March 1924) in J. Glaesemer, *Paul Klee. Die farbigen Werke in Kunstmuseum Bern*, 1976. Bern: Verlag Kornfeld, p. 138.

14   Rainer Maria Rilke, *The Duino Elegies*, translated by Stephen Garney and Jay Wilson, (New York: Harper Colophon Books, Harper and Row Publishers, 1972), p. 35.

15   The Greek discovery of the Golden Section probably came from the Babylonian development of the pentagram. It was the Italian mathematician Luca Pacioli who described the Golden Section as the *"divina proportione."* The term "Golden Section" was first used in 1830.

16   Dr. Helen Dow has been the scholar who has most strongly pursued this line of interpretation.

17   Dow, p. 90.

18   *Ibid.*, p. 92.

19   Interview with artist July 29, 1982.

20   W.B. Yeats, "The Second Coming," from *Michael Robartes and the Dancer*, 1921 in *W.B. Yeats: Selected Poetry*, (London: Pan Books in association with Macmillan London, 1974), pp. 99-100.

21   Wallace Stevens, "The Noble Rider and the Sound of Words," (1942), *The Necessary Angel*, (New York: Vintage Books, 1951), p. 6.

SIX: THE NOTION OF GRACE: SELF AND FAMILY AS SUBJECT

1   Heinz Ohff, "Provinziell wie Caspar David Friedrich," *Der Tagesspiegel/Feuilleton* (Berlin) 25 August 1971, s. 4.

2   T.S. Eliot, "East Coker," *Four Quartets* (London: Faber and Faber, 1979), p. 21.

3   See Dow, p. 207.

4   Interview with artist July 29, 1982.

5   Transcription of discussion at National Gallery of Canada with Rosemary Tovell and students from Ottawa University, February 18, 1977.

6   Interview with artist July 29, 1982.

7   Interview with artist July 28, 1982.

8   See note 5.

9   Interview with artist July 28, 1982.

10   Interview with artist July 29, 1982.

11   Dow, p. 135.

12   Harry Bruce, "Death, Art and Alex Colville," *Saturday Night* 87 (May 1972): 30 34.

13   Bertrand Russell, *The Autobiography of Bertrand Russell, Vol. I* (London: Allen and Unwin, 1967), p. 208.

PAINTING SITES

1. *At Grand Pré* 1982
2. *Night Walk* 1981
3. *Cyclist and Crow* 1981
4. *Seven Crows* 1980
5. *One Swallow* 1980
6. *Main Street* 1979
7. *Dog and Bridge* 1976
8. *Summer in Town* 1973
9. *Professor of Romance Languages* 1973
10. *Woman Carrying Canoe* 1972; *Sunrise* 1970
11. *Stop for Cows* 1967
12. *August* 1964
13. *Moon and Cow* 1963
14. *Elm Tree at Horton Landing* 1956
15. *Family and Rainstorm* 1955
16. *Three Sheep* 1954
17. *Visitors are Invited to Register* 1954
18. *Man on Verandah* 1953; *Headstand* 1982

CATALOGUE RAISONNÉ

COMPILED BY MARILYN SCHIFF

All works are on board unless otherwise indicated. In the measurements, height precedes width.

1 *Fitters "Break" Period* 1944
   Oil on canvas
   61.0 x 76.2 cm
   Signed lower right: *Alex Colville 1944*

   Canadian War Museum/National
      Museum of Man/National Museums of
      Canada

2 *Mechanical Transport Park* 1944
   Oil on canvas
   58.4 x 73.6 cm
   Signed lower right: *Alex Colville 1944*

   Canadian War Museum/National
      Museum of Man/National Museums of
      Canada

3 *Convoy in Yorkshire No. 2* 1944
   Oil on canvas
   76.3 x 102.0 cm
   Signed lower right: *Alex Colville 1944*

   Canadian War Museum/National
      Museum of Man/National Museums of
      Canada

4 *Lorries Under Trees* 1944
   Oil on canvas (unframed, unstretched)
   40.7 x 50.8 cm
   Signed lower right: *Alex Colville 1944*

   Canadian War Museum/National
      Museum of Man/National Museums of
      Canada

5 *Nissen Huts at Night* 1944
   Oil on canvas
   40.6 x 50.3 cm
   Signed lower right: *Alex Colville 44*

   Canadian War Museum/National
      Museum of Man/National Museums of
      Canada

6 *Tank Transporter Tractors No. 2* 1944
   Oil on canvas
   76.0 x 60.7 cm
   Signed lower right: *Alex Colville 1944*

   Canadian War Museum/National
      Museum of Man/National Museums of
      Canada

7 *HMCS Prince Henry in Corsica* 1944
   Oil on canvas
   76.2 x 101.6 cm
   Signed lower right: *Alex Colville 1944*

   Canadian War Museum/National
      Museum of Man/National Museums of
      Canada

8 *LCA's off Southern France* 1944
   Oil on canvas
   101.4 x 76.0 cm
   Signed lower right: *Alex Colville 1944*

   Canadian War Museum/National
      Museum of Man/National Museums of
      Canada

9 *Nijmegen Salient* 1944
   Oil on canvas
   76.4 x 102.0 cm
   Signed lower right: *Alex Colville 1944*

   Canadian War Museum/National
      Museum of Man/National Museums of
      Canada

10 *Tragic Landscape* 1945
   Oil on linen
   60.9 x 91.6 cm
   Signed lower right: *Alex Colville 45*

   Canadian War Museum/National
      Museum of Man/National Museums of
      Canada

11 *Bodies in a Grave, Belsen* 1945
   Oil on canvas
   76.2 x 101.3 cm
   Signed lower right: *Alex Colville 1945*

   Canadian War Museum/National
      Museum of Man/National Museums of
      Canada

12 *Messerschmitt* 1946
   Oil on canvas
   60.7 x 81.2 cm
   Signed lower right: *Alex Colville 1946*

   Canadian War Museum/National
      Museum of Man/National Museums of
      Canada

13 *Exhausted Prisoners* 1946
   Oil on canvas
   76.2 x 101.6 cm
   Signed lower left: *Alex Colville 1946*

   Canadian War Museum/National
      Museum of Man/National Museums of
      Canada

14 *Infantry Near Nijmegen, Holland* 1946
Oil on linen
101.6 x 122.0 cm
Signed lower left: *Alex Colville 1946*

Canadian War Museum/National
   Museum of Man/National Museums of
   Canada

15 *The Nijmegen Bridge, Holland* 1946
Oil on canvas
91.5 x 122.6 cm
Signed lower right: *Alex Colville 1946*

Canadian War Museum/National
   Museum of Man/National Museums of
   Canada

16 *Three Horses* 1946
Oil on canvas
50.8 x 66.0 cm
Signed lower right: *Alex Colville 1946*

Collection Art Gallery of Ontario,
   Purchase 1946

17 *Group of Horses* 1947
Oil on canvas
71.1 x 96.5 cm
Signed lower right: *Alex Colville 47*

Watson Gallery, Montreal

Whereabouts unknown

18 *Windmill and Farm* 1947
Oil
71.1 x 55.8 cm
Signed lower right: *Alex Colville 47*

Collection Dr. Elizabeth Harfenist

19 *Railroad over Marsh* 1947
Oil on canvas
60.9 x 81.2 cm
Signed lower right: *Alex Colville 47*
Watson Gallery, Montreal

Beaverbrook Art Gallery, Fredericton

20 *The History of Mount Allison* 1948
Egg tempera on gessoed wall
4.88 x 4.11 m

The mural was commissioned by Mount
Allison University for Tweedie Hall, the
student union building, through the
initiative of Norman Hessler, a local
businessman and Dr. Flemington, the
University's president. The composition
is centred on Charles F. Allison, the
university's founder, and the itinerant
preacher who converted him to
Methodism. The horse on which he is
seated is modelled after that in
Velazquez's *Surrender at Breda*. The
style of the work and its composition is
related to the mural paintings
commissioned under the WPA/FPA
projects in the United States of the 1930s.

Collection Owens Art Gallery, Mount
   Allison University, Sackville, NB

21 *Racetrack, Sackville* 1950
Oil
60.9 x 98.5 cm
Signed lower right: *Alex Colville*
R.G. Colville

Nova Scotia Art Bank

22 *Nude and Dummy* 1950
Glazed gum arabic emulsion
60.9 x 81.2 cm
Signed lower right: *Alex Colville 1950*

New Brunswick Museum, Saint John

23 *Seated Nude* 1950
Glazed tempera
50.8 x 40.6 cm
Signed lower right: *Alex Colville 1950*

Dr. Helen J. Dow

24 *Nudes on Shore* 1950
Glazed tempera
60.9 x 98.5 cm
Signed lower right: *Alex Colville 1950*

Beaverbrook Art Gallery, Fredericton

25 *Seated Nude* 1951
Glazed tempera
81.2 x 86.3 cm
Signed lower right: *Alex Colville 51*

The Artist

26 *Two Pacers* 1951
Glazed tempera
60.9 x 81.2 cm
Signed lower right: *Alex Colville 1951*
Dominion Galleries, Montreal

Private Collection, Ottawa

27 *Woman at Table* 1951
Glazed tempera
60.9 x 81.2 cm
Signed lower right: *Alex Colville 1951*
Dominion Galleries, Montreal

Private Collection, Ottawa

28 *Coastal Figure* 1951
Glazed tempera
60.9 x 139.7 cm
Signed lower right: *Alex Colville 1951*

The Artist

29 *Child and Dog* 1952
Glazed tempera
81.2 x 60.9 cm
Signed lower right: *Alex Colville 52*

National Gallery of Canada, Ottawa

30 *Four Figures on a Wharf* 1952
Casein tempera
35.5 x 71.1 cm
Signed lower right: *Alex Colville 52*

National Gallery of Canada, Ottawa

31 *Woman, Jockey and Horse* 1952
Glazed tempera
38.1 x 50.8 cm
Signed lower right: *Alex Colville 1952*
Hewitt Gallery, New York
Lincoln Kirstein

Private Collection

32 *Two Boys Playing* 1952
Glazed tempera
50.8 x 50.8 cm
Signed lower right: *Alex Colville 52*
T.H. Edwards, Montreal

Collection Mr. & Mrs. William Teron

33 *Girl on Piebald Horse* 1952
Glazed tempera
57.7 x 35.5 cm
Signed lower right: *Alex Colville 52*
Galerie Martin, Montreal
Private Collection
Dominion Galleries, Montreal

Collection Dr. & Mrs. Daniel Silver

34 *Woman, Man and Boat* 1952
Glazed tempera
31.7 x 48.9 cm
Signed lower right: *Alex Colville 52*

National Gallery of Canada, Ottawa

35 *Dog and Horse* 1953
Glazed tempera
38.1 x 50.8 cm
Signed lower right: *Alex Colville 1953*

Mr. & Mrs. J.L. Black, Sackville, NB

36 *Soldier and Girl at Station* 1953
Glazed tempera
40.6 x 60.9 cm
Signed lower left: *Alex Colville 1953*
Hewitt Gallery, New York

Private Collection

37 *Man on Verandah* 1953
Glazed tempera
38.1 x 50.8 cm
Signed lower right: *Alex Colville 1953*
Dominion Galleries, Montreal

The man in CR 37 is based on Rhoda
Colville's stepfather, Mr. Cox. The setting
is at Evangeline Beach near Wolfville.

Collection G.H. Southam

38 *Three Girls on a Wharf* 1953
Glazed tempera
41.3 x 25.4 cm
Signed lower right: *Alex Colville 53*
Dominion Galleries, Montreal
Mrs. P. Cushing
L. Drummond
James Henwood

Collection Mr. & Mrs. Christopher
Ondaatje

39 *Racer* 1954
Casein tempera
45.7 cm diameter
Signed lower right: *Alex Colville 54*
Donnelley Erdman

The man in CR 39 is based on a
photograph of Rhoda Colville's father,
Mr. C.H. Wright. Colville never met Mr.
Wright, a builder and developer, who
was killed in 1928. The picture was, in
part, developed from Colville's reading
of Erich Maria Remarque's novel *Arc de
Triomphe*.

Private Collection

40 *Prize Bull* 1954
Casein tempera
30.4 x 38.1 cm
Signed lower right: *Alex Colville 54*
M. Lesser

CR 40 is a preparatory painting for *Cattle
Show*, 1955 (CR 48). It was made from a
sketch done at the Atlantic Winter Fair in
Amherst. Concerning the drawing
Colville wrote, "I told my barber in
Sackville NB about being in the stall with
the bull, who behaved like a spaniel dog.
The barber, George Chapman, whom I
knew very well, told me that I might have
been killed, as bulls are unpredictable.
An artist's life is full of hazards." (Letter
to Robert W. Manuge, Halifax, February
13, 1982).

Manuge Gallery, Halifax

41 *Nude on Rug* 1954
Casein tempera
38.1 x 30.4 cm
Signed lower right: *Alex Colville 54*
Mr. and Mrs. J. Loeb

Private Collection, Ottawa

42 *Woman on Wharf* 1954
Casein tempera
24.1 x 15.2 cm
Signed lower right: *Alex Colville 54*
Oliver B. Jennings, New York

Dr. Helen J. Dow

43 *Horse and Train* 1954
Glazed tempera
40.0 x 53.3 cm
Signed lower right: *Alex Colville 1954*

Art Gallery of Hamilton, Gift of
    Dominion Foundries and Steel,
    Limited, 1957

44 *Visitors are Invited to Register* 1954
Casein tempera
35.5 x 48.2 cm
Signed lower right: *Alex Colville 54*

Mendel Art Gallery Collection, Gift of the
    Canadian National Exhibition
    Association

45 *Three Sheep* 1954
Casein tempera
30.4 x 49.1 cm
Signed lower right: *Alex Colville 54*
Hewitt Gallery, New York

Lincoln Kirstein

46 *Two Riveters* 1954
Casein tempera
50.8 x 38.1 cm
Signed lower right: *Alex Colville*

University of Guelph Collection,
    MacDonald Stewart Art Centre,
    Guelph, Gift of the Ontario Veterinary
    College Alumni Association, 1972

47 *Child with Accordion* 1954
Casein tempera
38.1 x 38.1 cm
Signed lower right: *Alex Colville 1954*
Dominion Galleries, Montreal

Private Collection

48 *Cattle Show* 1955
Glazed oil emulsion
60.9 x 98.7 cm
Signed lower right: *Alex Colville 1955*
Hewitt Gallery, New York

The setting of CR 48, for which CR 40 was
a preparatory sketch, is the Winter Fair
in Amherst which Colville attended each
year when he was living in Sackville.

Private Collection

49 *Family and Rainstorm* 1955
Glazed tempera
53.3 x 71.1 cm
Signed lower right: *Alex Colville 1955*

National Gallery of Canada, Ottawa

50 *Three Shepherds* 1955
Casein tempera
53.3 x 71.1 cm
Signed lower right: *Alex Colville 1955*
Hewitt Gallery, New York

CR 50 was commissioned by Hallmark
Cards Incorporated for use on a
Christmas card. The card was not
published.

Hallmark Cards Incorporated

51 *Illustration for "The Ball Poem" by John
    Berryman* 1956
Casein tempera
22.8 x 15.2 cm
Signed lower right: *Alex Colville 56*

Private Collection, Montreal

52 *Elm Tree at Horton Landing* 1956
Oil emulsion
121.9 x 91.4 cm
Signed lower right: *Alex Colville 1956*

Collection Art Gallery of Ontario, Gift
    from the McLean Foundation, 1958

53 *Woman at Clothesline* 1956-7
Glazed oil emulsion
121.9 x 91.4 cm
Signed lower right: *Alex Colville 1956-7*

National Gallery of Canada, Ottawa

54 *Children in Tree* 1957
Casein tempera
47.6 x 54.6 cm
Signed lower right: *Alex Colville 1957*

CR 54 was made in preparation for a
mural for the Canadian Pavilion at the
Brussels World Fair of 1958. The mural
was not, in the result, painted. CR 54 is
the only picture in which all four of
Colville's children are included.

C I L Inc.

55 *Couple on Beach* 1957
Casein tempera
68.5 x 91.4 cm
Signed lower right: *Alex Colville 1957*
Laing Galleries, Toronto

National Gallery of Canada, Ottawa

56 *Hound in Field* 1958
Casein tempera
76.2 x 101.6 cm
Signed lower right: *Alex Colville 58*
Laing Galleries, Toronto

National Gallery of Canada, Ottawa

57 *Child Skipping* 1958
Oil and synthetic resin
60.9 x 45.7 cm
Signed lower right: *Alex Colville 1958*

Private Collection, Toronto

58 *Swimming Race* 1958
Oil and synthetic resin
60.9 x 98.5 cm
Signed lower right: *Alex Colville 1958*
Lincoln Kirstein

National Gallery of Canada, Ottawa

59 *Dog, Boy and St. John River* 1958
Oil and synthetic resin
60.9 x 81.3 cm
Signed lower right: *Alex Colville 1958*

CR 59 was commissioned by *Maclean's
Magazine* to illustrate an article by Hugh
MacLennan in a series "The Rivers Of
Canada." The painting was reproduced
in the magazine which included
MacLennan's article "The Languid and
Lovely St. John," *Maclean's* 72 (July 4,
1959), p. 23.

London Regional Art Gallery, London,
    Ontario, Canada

60 *Milk Truck* 1959
Oil and synthetic resin
45.7 x 45.7 cm
Signed lower right: *Alex Colville 1959*

C-I-L Inc.

61 *Circus Woman* 1959-60
Oil and synthetic resin
66.0 x 76.2 cm
Signed lower right: *Alex Colville 1959-60*
Banfer Gallery, New York

Dr. Helen J. Dow

62 *Dog, Boy and School Bus* 1960
Oil and synthetic resin
68.5 x 59.3 cm
Signed lower right: *Alex Colville 1960*
Banfer Gallery, New York

Private Collection

63 *Mr. Wood in April* 1960
Oil and synthetic resin
60.9 x 91.4 cm
Signed lower right: *Alex Colville 1960*

Mr. and Mrs. J.W. Black

64 *Athletes* 1960-61
Oil and synthetic resin
1.52 m x 2.42 m (triptych)

In addition to painting CR 64, Colville
also designed the colour scheme for the
Athletic Centre.

Collection Owens Art Gallery, Mount
    Allison University, Sackville, NB

65 *Ocean Limited* 1962
Oil and synthetic resin
68.5 x 119.3 cm
Signed lower right: *Alex Colville 1962*
Banfer Gallery, New York

Collection William A.M. Burden & Co.

66 *Departure* 1962
Oil and synthetic resin
45.7 x 66.0 cm
Signed lower right: *Alex Colville 1962*

Kestner-Gesellschaft, Hanover, West
    Germany

67 *Swimmer* 1962
Egg tempera
53.3 x 71.1 cm
Signed lower right: *Alex Colville 1962*
Banfer Gallery, New York

Dr. Helen J. Dow

68   *Moon and Cow* 1963
Oil and synthetic resin
68.5 x 91.4 cm
Signed lower right: *Alex Colville 1963*
Banfer Gallery, New York

Donnelley Erdman, Aspen, Colorado

69   *June Noon* 1963
Acrylic polymer emulsion
76.2 x 76.2 cm
Signed lower right: *Alex Colville 1963*
Marlborough Fine Art, London
Donnelley Erdman
Fischer Fine Art, London

Private Collection, Düsseldorf, Germany

70   *Woman and Terrier* 1963
Acrylic polymer emulsion
60.9 cm diameter
Signed at bottom: *Alex Colville 1963*
Marlborough Fine Art, London

Private Collection

71   *Church and Horse* 1964
Acrylic polymer emulsion
55.3 x 68.5 cm
Signed lower right: *Alex Colville 1964*
Isaacs Gallery, Toronto

The Montreal Museum of Fine Arts,
Purchase, Horsley and Annie
Townsend Bequest and Anonymous
Donor

72   *Skater* 1964
Acrylic polymer emulsion
113.0 x 69.8 cm
Signed lower right: *Alex Colville 1964*

The Museum of Modern Art, New York,
Gift of R.H. Donnelley Erdman (by
exchange), 1965

73   *August* 1964
Acrylic polymer emulsion
42.1 x 86.3 cm
Signed lower right: *Alex Colville 1964*
Lady Brinkman, Ottawa

Private Collection, Ottawa

74   *To Prince Edward Island* 1965
Acrylic polymer emulsion
60.9 x 91.4 cm
Signed lower right: *Alex Colville 1965*

National Gallery of Canada, Ottawa

75   *Truck Stop* 1966
Acrylic polymer emulsion
91.4 x 91.4 cm
Marlborough Fine Art, London
Dr. P. Ludwig, Aachen

Museum Ludwig, Köln

76   *Crow Up Early* 1966
Acrylic polymer emulsion
45.7 x 68.5 cm
Arthur Fouks, Vancouver
Thomas Gibson, Ltd., London
Fischer Fine Art, London

Private Collection

77   *Stop for Cows* 1967
Acrylic polymer emulsion
60.9 x 91.4 cm
Fischer Fine Art, London

Museum Boymans-van Beuningen,
Rotterdam, the Netherlands

78   *Pacific* 1967
Acrylic polymer emulsion
53.3 x 53.3 cm
Marlborough Fine Art, London

Private Collection, Toronto

79   *My Father With His Dog* 1968
Acrylic polymer emulsion
93.6 cm diameter
Fischer Fine Art, London

Private Collection, Ottobrunn, West
Germany

80   *Road Work* 1969
Acrylic polymer emulsion
53.3 x 83.6 cm
Marlborough Fine Art, London
P. Bronfman, Montreal
Waddington Galleries, Toronto

Mr. & Mrs. Jules Loeb

81   *Cow and Calf* 1969
Acrylic polymer emulsion
40.0 x 53.3 cm
Marlborough Fine Art, London

Private Collection, Düsseldorf, West
Germany

82   *Sign and Harrier* 1970
Acrylic polymer emulsion
83.6 cm diameter
Fischer Fine Art, London

Musée national d'art moderne – Centre
Georges Pompidou

83 *May Day* 1970
Acrylic polymer emulsion
43.1 x 43.1 cm
Fischer Fine Art, London

CR 83 was based on an Associated Press
photograph of Barbara Lovell, daughter
of James Lovell, the commander of
Apollo 12, during the efforts to bring the
crippled spacecraft back to earth.

Collection of the Lynnwood Arts Centre,
Simcoe, Ontario

84 *Owl* 1970
Acrylic polymer emulsion
22.8 x 30.4 cm
Fischer Fine Art, London

Kitchener-Waterloo Art Gallery

85 *Snowstorm* 1971
Acrylic polymer emulsion
22.8 x 30.4 cm
Fischer Fine Art, London

Private Collection

86 *January* 1971
Acrylic polymer emulsion
60.9 x 81.2 cm
Fischer Fine Art, London

Collection of Toronto Dominion Bank,
Toronto

87 *The River Spree* 1971
Acrylic polymer emulsion
60.0 x 104.0 cm
Fischer Fine Art, London
Dr. P. Ludwig, Aachen

Museum der moderner Kunst, Vienna
Leihgabe Sammlung Ludwig/Aachen

88 *Woman Carrying Canoe* 1972
Acrylic polymer emulsion
48.2 x 83.8 cm
Fischer Fine Art, London
Gallery Moos, Toronto

Private Collection

89 *Woman in Bathtub* 1973
Acrylic polymer emulsion
86.3 x 86.3 cm
Fischer Fine Art, London
Private Collection, Rome
Fischer Fine Art, London

Collection Art Gallery of Ontario,
Purchase with assistance from
Wintario, 1978

90 *Summer in Town* 1973
Acrylic polymer emulsion
30.4 x 45.7 cm
Fischer Fine Art, London
Galerie Royale, Vancouver
James Henwood

Mr. & Mrs. Donald MacKenzie

91 *Professor of Romance Languages* 1973
Acrylic polymer emulsion
68.5 x 91.4 cm
Fischer Fine Art, London
Manuge Galleries, Halifax

Mr. & Mrs. Irving Ungerman

92 *Labours of the Months – January* 1974
Acrylic polymer emulsion
20.3 x 20.3 cm
Galerie Royale

Private Collection, Edmonton

93 *Labours of the Months – February* 1974
Acrylic polymer emulsion
20.3 x 20.3 cm
Private Collection, Vancouver
Downstairs Gallery, Edmonton

Private Collection, Edmonton

94 *Labours of the Months – March* 1974
Acrylic polymer emulsion
20.3 x 20.3 cm
Art Emporium, Vancouver

Private Collection, Victoria

95 *Labours of the Months – April* 1974
Acrylic polymer emulsion
20.3 x 20.3 cm
Downstairs Gallery, Edmonton
Private Collection, Edmonton
Downstairs Gallery, Edmonton

Private Collection, Edmonton

96 *Labours of the Months – May* 1974
Acrylic polymer emulsion
20.3 x 20.3 cm
Art Emporium, Vancouver

Private Collection, Calgary

97 *Labours of the Months – June* 1974
Acrylic polymer emulsion
20.3 x 20.3 cm
Art Emporium, Vancouver

Private Collection, Calgary

98 *Labours of the Months–July* 1974
Acrylic polymer emulsion
20.3 x 20.3 cm
Mira Godard Gallery

Private Collection, Winnipeg

99 *Labours of the Months–August* 1974
Acrylic polymer emulsion
20.3 x 20.3 cm
Mira Godard Gallery

Private Collection, Calgary

100 *Labours of the Months–September* 1974
Acrylic polymer emulsion
20.3 x 20.3 cm
Mira Godard Gallery

Private Collection, London, Ontario

101 *Labours of the Months–October* 1974
Acrylic polymer emulsion
20.3 x 20.3 cm
Fischer Fine Art, London

Private Collection, Regina

102 *Labours of the Months–November* 1974
Acrylic polymer emulsion
20.3 x 20.3 cm
Mira Godard Gallery

Private Collection, Montreal

103 *Labours of the Months–December* 1974
Acrylic polymer emulsion
20.3 x 20.3 cm
Galerie Royale, Vancouver

Private Collection, Nanaimo

104 *The River Thames* 1974
Acrylic polymer emulsion
76.2 x 76.2 cm
Fischer Fine Art, London

Mr. & Mrs. J.H. Clark

105 *Harbour* 1975
Acrylic polymer emulsion
33.0 x 53.3 cm
Fischer Fine Art, London
Galerie Pudelko, Bonn

Private Collection

106 *Looking Up* 1975
Acrylic polymer emulsion
30.4 x 26.3 cm
Fischer Fine Art, London

CR 106 and 129 were developed from
drawings first related to CR 74, *To Prince
Edward Island*

Private Collection

107 *Dog and Bridge* 1976
Acrylic polymer emulsion
86.3 x 86.3 cm
Fischer Fine Art, London

Mr. & Mrs. J.H. Clark

108 *Crow and Sheep* 1976
Acrylic polymer emulsion
30.4 cm diameter
Fischer Fine Art, London
Manuge Galleries, Halifax

Private Collection, Vancouver

109 *In the Woods* 1976
Acrylic polymer emulsion
34.2 x 59.3 cm
Fischer Fine Art, London
Galerie Royale, Vancouver
Mira Godard Gallery

Private Collection, Montreal

110 *Laser* 1976
Acrylic polymer emulsion
57.7 x 100.0 cm
Fischer Fine Art, London
Dr. P. Ludwig

Staatliche Museen zu Berlin, DDR

111 *Refrigerator* 1977
Acrylic polymer emulsion
120.0 x 74.0 cm
Fischer Fine Art, London

Private Collection

112 *Berlin Bus* 1978
Acrylic polymer emulsion
53.4 x 53.4 cm
Fischer Fine Art, London
Mira Godard Gallery

Private Collection

113 *Dog and Priest* 1978
Acrylic polymer emulsion
52.0 x 90.0 cm
Fischer Fine Art, London
Mira Godard Gallery

Collection Mr. & Mrs. William Teron

114 *Main Street* 1979
Acrylic polymer emulsion
61.0 x 86.2 cm
Fischer Fine Art, London
Equinox Gallery, Vancouver

Consolidated-Bathurst Inc.

115 *Swimming Dog and Canoe* 1979
Acrylic polymer emulsion
53.4 x 119.4 cm
Fischer Fine Art, London

Private Collection, Geneva

116 *One Swallow* 1980
Acrylic polymer emulsion
99.0 x 40.8 cm
Fischer Fine Art, London

CR 116 is based on the proverb "One
swallow does not make a summer" for
which Brewers *Dictionary of Phrase
and Fable* gives the following definition,
"You are not to suppose summer has
come to stay just because you have seen
a swallow; nor that the troubles of life
are over because you have surmounted
one difficulty."

From the Collection of Mrs. John Rykert

117 *Target Pistol and Man* 1980
Acrylic polymer emulsion
60.0 x 60.0 cm
Fischer Fine Art, London
Kenneth Heffel Fine Art, Vancouver

Private Collection, Calgary

118 *Seven Crows* 1980
Acrylic polymer emulsion
60.0 x 120.0 cm
Fischer Fine Art, London

Ross B. Eddy

119 *Cyclist and Crow* 1981
Acrylic polymer emulsion
70.6 x 100.0 cm
Fischer Fine Art, London

Collection Lavalin Inc.

120 *Night Walk* 1981
Acrylic polymer emulsion
45.7 x 45.7 cm

The figure in the picture is, as in CR 127,
an evocation of Colville's mother's
father.

Fischer Fine Art, London

121 *Headstand* 1982
Acrylic polymer emulsion
66.0 x 40.8 cm

Fischer Fine Art, London

122 *At Grand Pré* 1982
Acrylic polymer emulsion
68.0 x 96.0 cm

Fischer Fine Art, London

PRINTS: 1955-1982

123 *After Swimming* 1955
Serigraph on paper, edition 27
63.5 x 38.1 cm
Signed and dated: *Alex Colville 1955*

124 *Cat on Fence* 1956
Serigraph on paper, edition 20
53.3 x 71.1 cm
Signed and dated: *Alex Colville 1956*

125 *High Diver* 1957
Serigraph on paper, edition 20
99.5 x 44.4 cm
Signed and dated: *Alex Colville 1957*

126 *Woman with Brassiere* 1958
Serigraph on paper, edition 16
36.7 x 33.8 cm
Signed and dated: *Alex Colville 1958*

127 *Ballad of the Fox Hunter* 1959
Serigraph on paper, edition 25
4 panels; 45.7 x 25.4 cm each
Signed and dated: *Alex Colville 1959* on
    each panel

CR 127 comprises a set of four
serigraphs illustrating the poem by W.B.
Yeats. Colville wrote out and printed
three verses of the poem under each of
the images. The man in the images is an
evocation of his mother's father.

128 *Dog With Bone* 1960-61
Serigraph on paper, edition 20
75.9 x 53.3 cm
Signed and dated: *Alex Colville 1961*

129 *Boat and Marker* 1964
Serigraph on paper, edition 17
48.2 x 48.2 cm
Signed and dated: *Alex Colville 1964*

130 *Ravens at the Dump* 1965
Serigraph on paper, edition 19
30.5 x 68.6 cm
Numbered, signed and dated: *Alex
    Colville 1965*

131 *Snowplow* 1967
Serigraph on paper, edition 20
61.0 x 81.2 cm
Numbered, signed and dated: *Alex
    Colville 1967*

132 *Running Dog* 1968
Serigraph on paper, edition 43
35.2 x 61.0 cm
Numbered, signed and dated: *Alex
    Colville 1968*

133 *Snow* 1969
Serigraph on paper, edition 70
61.0 x 45.7 cm
Numbered, signed and dated: *Alex Colville 1969*

The origin of CR 133 is found in Robert Lowell's *Imitations*. Lowell's book is a collection of creative translations of a wide range of poems. Colville's serigraph refers to Lowell's version of *Ballad for the Dead Ladies* from *Le grand testament* by François Villon (1431?-1463). At the end of each of the four verses is the refrain, "Oh where is last year's snow." (See Robert Lowell, *Imitations* (New York: Farrar, Straus and Giroux, 1961), p. 15.

134 *Sunrise* 1970
Serigraph on paper, edition 70
30.5 x 61.0 cm
Numbered, signed and dated: *Alex Colville 1970*

135 *Crow with Silver Spoon* 1972
Serigraph on paper, edition 70
45.7 cm diameter
Numbered, signed and dated: *Alex Colville 1972*

136 *Border Collie* 1972
Serigraph on paper, edition 500
11.4 x 11.4 cm
Numbered, signed and dated: *Alex Colville 1972*

137 *Sleeper* 1975
Serigraph on Harumi board, edition 70
43.0 x 53.4 cm
Numbered, signed and dated: *Alex Colville 1975*

138 *Heron* 1977
Serigraph on Harumi board, edition 70
33.0 x 86.0 cm
Numbered, signed and dated: *Alex Colville 1977*

139 *Prize Cow* 1977
Serigraph on Harumi board, edition 70
43.0 cm diameter
Numbered, signed and dated: *Alex Colville 1977*

140 *Hotel Maid* 1978
Serigraph on Rising board, edition 100; 75 numbered in arabic numerals, 25 numbered in roman numerals.
24.1 x 20.0 cm
Numbered, signed and dated: *Alex Colville 1978*

141 *Labours of the Months* 1978
Lithograph, boxed set of 12; edition 100; 75 numbered in arabic numerals, 25 numbered in roman numerals.
20.0 x 20.0 cm each
Numbered, signed and dated: *Alex Colville 1978*

Colville was approached by the Olivetti company to produce a series on the months for reproduction as a calendar. The project was subsequently abandoned but the images, developed from the paintings (CR 92-103), were made into a set of lithographs issued as a boxed set and published by Fischer Fine Art and Mira Godard Gallery. Each of the boxed sets included the serigraph *Hotel Maid* (CR 140).

142 *Cat and Artist* 1979
Serigraph on Harumi board, edition 70
23.1 cm diameter
Numbered, signed and dated: *Alex Colville 1979*

143 *New Moon* 1980
Serigraph on Rising board, edition 70
36.0 x 45.0 cm
Numbered, signed and dated: *Alex Colville 1980*

144 *Morning* 1981
Serigraph on Harumi board, edition 70
54.6 cm diameter
Numbered, signed and dated: *Alex Colville 1981*

145 *Woman, Dog and Canoe* 1982
Serigraph on Harumi board, edition 70
43.1 x 69.8 cm
Numbered, signed and dated: *Alex Colville 1982*

CAST WORKS

146 Coin Designs for Centennial Year 1965
Silver, nickel, copper (minted 1967)
Various sizes

Colville was commissioned in 1965, after winning a nationwide competition, to design the reverse side of a set of coins to commemorate the centenary of Confederation. The coins were minted in 1967. He made both the measured drawings and plaster models from which the dies were cast. The six coins are: 1 cent–a pigeon; 5 cents–a rabbit; 10 cents–a mackerel; 25 cents–a wildcat; 50 cents–a wolf; 1 dollar–a Canada goose.

In a statement issued as a press release from the Department of Finance April 20, 1966 (see Dow pp. 208-209), Colville explained his choice of subjects:

> In considering what would be most suitable for Centennial coins, I decided that only the world of nature would provide themes with sufficient depth of meaning. It is a question of finding images which are worthy and appropriate ... images which will express not merely some particular time, place, or event, but a whole century of Canada, and even more; natural creatures provide this enduring and meaningful continuum....1 would even say that nature is a kind of golden measure against which human acts are measured....

147 *Fox and Hedgehog* 1972
Open 18 carat gold medallion on chain, edition 12
4.7 cm width
Numbered, signed and dated: *Alex Colville 1972*

Colville was commissioned by S.J. Phillips Ltd. and Fischer Fine Art to design a piece of jewellery. The subject Colville chose was taken from the ancient Greek proverb from Archilochus of Paros, "The fox knows many things, but the hedgehog knows one big thing." Colville's specific point of reference for the subject was based on Isaiah Berlin's essay on Tolstoy's view of history; see "The Hedgehog and the Fox." *Russian Thinkers* (Harmondsworth: Penguin Books Ltd., 1979), pp. 22-81.

148 *Governor General's Medal* 1975
Gold
5.2 cm diameter

Colville was commissioned to produce the design for the medal commemorating Governor General and Mrs. Léger. Recipients of the Governor Generals' medals are principally outstanding graduates of high schools, colleges, and universities. The medals are minted in bronze, silver, and gold and awarded according to academic level. The tradition of the awards was established by Lord Dufferin in 1873.

STUDENT AND DESTROYED WORKS

149 *Prospect, NS* 1939
Oil on composition board
30.5 x 39.7 cm
Signed lower right: *Alex Colville 1939*
Miss Marion Gilroy

Vancouver Art Gallery

150 *Peggy's Cove, NS* 1940
Oil on beaverboard
29.8 x 40 cm
Signed lower right: *Alex Colville 1940*

Dr. Helen J. Dow

151 *St. John River near Woodstock, NB* 1941
Oil on canvas
91.4 x 71.1 cm
Signed lower right: *Alex Colville 1941*

Private Collection, Santa Barbara, California

152 *Wounded Soldier in North Africa* 1941
Oil and beeswax on beaverboard
2.43 x 1.21 m
Destroyed 1946 or 1947

153 *Departure* 1942
Oil and beeswax on beaverboard
1.22 x 2.74 m
Destroyed 1946 or 1947

154 *Self-Portrait* 1942
Oil on canvas
Dimensions unknown
Signed lower left: *Colville '42*
Destroyed

155 *Galloping Horse* 1954
Wire, cord, painted plaster
27.9 cm long
Destroyed

156 *Backdrop for Vesper Service* 1954
Casein on wrapping paper
2.44 x 9.75 m
Destroyed

SELECTED BIBLIOGRAPHY

COMPILED BY MARILYN SCHIFF

ARTIST'S STATEMENTS

1951   *My Experience as a Painter and Some General Views of Art*. Address given at New Brunswick Museum, St. John, NB (Mimeograph transcription by Mount Allison Federated Alumni, Sackville, NB) (Reprinted in Dow, pp. 203-8).

1961   "Letter on Architecture," *Canadian Art* 8 (Spring 1951): 121.

"18 Canadian Printmakers," *Canadian Art* 18 (March/April 1961): 102-3.

"Canadian Conference of the Arts," *Canadian Art* 18 (September/October 1961): 291.

1966   Statement on Centennial Coins. Press Release, Department of Finance, Government of Canada, (April 20, 1966). (Reprinted in Dow, pp. 208-9).

1967   "Alex Colville, Wolfeville [sic] Nova Scotia," *Statements–18 Canadian Artists*, Regina, Saskatchewan, Norman Mackenzie Art Gallery. (Reprinted in Dow, pp. 209-10).

1973   "Some Thoughts About My Painting," Unpublished Statement. (29 November 1973).

1975   "Rome and the Bull-Dozer," *Preserving Canada's Heritage*, Symposium. Royal Society of Canada, Ottawa. (7, 8 October 1975).

1981   Convocation Address, Memorial University of Newfoundland. (Unpublished) St. John's, Newfoundland. (31 October 1981).

"An Artist in Canada," Brockington Lecture. Queen's University, Kingston, Ont. (16 November 1981). Published *Kingston Whig-Standard Magazine*, 11 November 1981.

BOOKS

Ayre, Robert. *The Arts in Canada: A Stock-Taking at Mid-Century*. "Painting." Toronto: Macmillan Co., 1958.

Clermont, Ghislain. *Alex Colville: une introduction à l'homme et à l'oeuvre*. Montreal: Université de Montréal, Master's Thesis, 1971 (Unpublished).

Colville, Alex. *Alex Colville: Diary of a War Artist*. Compiled by Graham Metson and Cheryl Maclean. Halifax: Nimbus Publishing Limited, 1981.

Dow, Helen. *The Art of Alex Colville*. Toronto: McGraw-Hill Ryerson Limited, 1972.

Duval, Paul. *High Realism in Canada*. Toronto: Clarke Irwin & Co. Limited, 1974.

Harper, J. Russell. *Painting in Canada: a history*. (Second edition) Toronto: University of Toronto Press, 1977.

Hubbard, Robert Hamilton. *An Anthology of Canadian Art*. Toronto: Oxford University Press, 1960.

Kilbourn, Elizabeth. *Great Canadian Painting: A Century of Art*. Toronto: Canadian Centennial Publishing Co., 1966.

Reid, Dennis. *A Concise History of Canadian Painting*. Toronto: Oxford University Press, 1973.

Withrow, William. *Contemporary Canadian Painting*. Toronto: McClelland and Stewart Limited, 1972.

PERIODICALS AND REVIEWS

Abadie, Daniel. "L'hyperréalisme." *Le Monde* (Paris), Autumn 1973, p. 5.

——. "L'Étrange solitude d'Alex Colville." *XXth Siècle*, no. 45 (1975), pp. 117-120.

Askew, Rual. "Canada's Art is Vigorous." *Dallas Morning News*, 14 September 1958. (Review, Dallas Museum of Contemporary Arts).

Bagnell, Kenneth. "The Uncanny Realism of Alex Colville." *Reader's Digest*, 107 (August, 1975): 56-62.

Balfour Bowen, Lisa. "Alex Colville's War: Symphonies of Colour." *Toronto Star*, 25 October 1981, p. B11. (Review of *Alex Colville: Diary of a War Artist*.)

Barnard, Elissa. "A Terrible, Stark Beauty in Colville's Drawings of War." *Halifax Mail Star*, 16 February 1981. (Review of War Art Exhibition, Mt. St. Vincent, Halifax.)

Barnard, Murray. "How a Recluse From New Brunswick Scored on the New York Market." *Maclean's* (Toronto), 76, 16 November 1963, p. 82.

——. "He Paints a World You've Never Seen." *Star Weekly* (Toronto), 27 August 1966.

Bowen, Donald. "An Artist's View of Some Contemporary Commonwealth Painters." *Journal of The Royal Society of Arts* (October 1971): 778-781.

Bruce, Harry. "Death, Art and Alex Colville." *Saturday Night* 87 (May 1972): 30-34.

——. "Beside the Shadow of the Raven." *Canadian Magazine*, 15 January 1977, pp. 10-13.

——. "Celebrating Life and Freezing Magical Moments." *The 4th Estate* (Halifax), 17 February 1977, pp. 10-11.

——. "Rarer Reality." *Canadian Magazine*, 26 November 1977, pp. 18-21.

——. " 'The Most Important Realist Painter of the Western World'." *Atlantic Insight* 3 (December 1981): 42-48.

Brunet-Weinmann, Monique. "Alex Colville ou la dimension mythique du monde." *Vie des Arts* 23 (Printemps 1979): 67-68.

Carpenter, Ken. "Toronto–Alex Colville at Godard." *Art in America* 67 (January/February 1979): 145.

Casselman, Karen. "Colville, Pratt, Forrestall are Fine, but What About Morton, Climo, McKay?", *Atlantic Insight* (May 1979): 52-53.

Chicoine, René. "Lyrisme canadien, national, enregistré et limité." *Le Devoir* (Montreal), 18 September 1957.

Cork, Richard. "70 Years' Ferment–But it Leaves this Painter Cold." *Evening Standard* (London), 20 January 1970.

De Santana, H. "Where Discipline Becomes Art." *Maclean's*, 25 September 1978, pp. 3-6.

Dow, Helen J. "The Magic Realism of Alex Colville." *Art Journal* 24 (Summer 1965): 318-329.

——. "Alex Colville, A Modern Poussin." *Journal of Canadian Studies* 6 (November 1971): 54-62.

——. "Alex Colville An Image-Maker." *British Journal of Aesthetics* 22 (July 1972): 290-302.

Duval, Paul. "Review, Laing Galleries." *Toronto Telegram*, 1 November 1958.

——. "He Is Winning Against the Grain." *The Telegram* (Toronto), 14 September 1963. (Dunn International Award)

Edmunston, Wayne. "The Raymond Chandler of Art." *The Vancouver Sun*, 30 July 1977, p. 37.

Ehrlich, Richard. "The Impact of the Equivocal." *Art and Artists* 12 (August 1977): 44-46.

Fitzgerald, John. "At $20,000 for a Single Painting, Alex Knows His Time is Valuable." *The Gazette* (Montreal), 14 October 1978.

Fulford, Robert. "IV Biennial Exhibition of Canadian Art." *Canadian Art* 18 (July/August 1961): 278.

——. "People Who Live in Cities are Heroes." *Daily Star* (Toronto), 19 January 1966.

Furtado, Raul. "Alex Colville, The Magic of the Commonplace." *Art Voices*, 4 (Fall 1965): 102.

Green, Robin. "Medal Designed By Alex Colville." *Globe and Mail* (Toronto), 3 March 1978.

Greenwood, Michael. "Alex Colville." *artscanada* 33 (December/January 1977): 34-37.

Hammock, Virgil. "Alex Colville: La Perfection dans le Réalisme." *Vie des Arts* 21 (August 1976): 14-21; 86-89.

Hutchings, Patrick A.E. "The Celebrative Realism of Alex Colville." *Westerly.* (August 1965): 55-65.

——. "Realism, Surrealism and Celebration: The Paintings of Alex Colville in the Collection of the National Gallery of Canada." *National Gallery of Canada Bulletin*, no. 8 (1966), pp. 16-28.

Inglis, Grace. "Colville's Bearing Speaks of Self-Discipline." *Hamilton Spectator*, 6 October 1979.

Innes, Lorna. "The War Art of Alex Colville is a Moving, Personal Record." *Halifax Mail Star*, 26 September 1981. (Review of *Alex Colville: Diary of a War Artist*.)

James, Geoffrey. "Obsessive Images." *Time* 2 February 1970, pp. 8-10.

Kattan, Naim. "La Rose est une Fleur." *Le Macleans* (October 1974): 14-28; 34.

Kieran, Sheila. "Alex Colville: Haunting Visions." *Star Weekly* (Toronto), 21 June 1969, pp. 16-19.

——. "The Art of Alex Colville." *Canadian Forum* (February 1974): 42-43.

Kirstein, Lincoln. "Alex Colville." *Canadian Art* 15 (August 1958): 216-219.

Kipphoff, Petra. "Alex Colville." *Zeit magazin* 2 October 1970, s. 52-54.

Littman, Sol. "The Chilling World of Colville." *Sunday Star* (Toronto), 24 September 1978.

Lynton, Norbert. "Reaching for the Moon." *The Guardian* (London), 30 January 1970.

MacKeeman, Karl. "Alex Colville–Printmaking in Nova Scotia." *Artmagazine* 18 (March/April 1977): 19.

Macrae, Scott. "An Artist in the Realm of Morality." *Vancouver Sun*, 5 February 1974.

Marteau, Robert. "Une planète nommée Colville." *Le Devoir* (Montreal), 4 November 1978, p. 32.

McCarthy, Pearl. "Colville And Works Both Rarities." *Globe and Mail*, 25 October 1958. (Review of Laing Galleries.)

Melville, Robert. "For Real." *The New Statesman* (London), 23 January 1970, pp. 126-127.

———. "A Note on Alex Colville." *Art International* 21 (May/June 1977): 32-34; 39-41.

Millier, Arthur. "Review, Lane Galleries Group Show." *Los Angeles Times*, 11 August 1957.

Mollins, Carl. "Alex Colville. Une renommée mondiale." *Le Droit* (Ottawa), 16 July 1977.

Mullaly, Terence. "Turning Point in the History of Art." *Daily Telegraph* (London), 19 January 1970.

———. "Alex Colville Arrests and Holds Attention." *Daily Telegraph* (London), 28 June 1977.

G.T.M. "Review, Hewitt Show." *Art News* (April 1955).

A.N. "Review–Alex Colville-Hewitt Gallery." *Art Digest*, 1 March 1955.

Neesham, Robin. "Painting: After the Seven, What?" *Chronicle-Herald, Mail Star* (Halifax), Centennial Supplement, "Century 1867-1967," 13 February 1967, p. 56.

O'Brien, Paddy. "Surrealism." *Canadian Art* 20 (November/December 1963): 350.

Ohff, Heinz. "Provinziell wie Caspar David Friedrich." *Der Tagesspiegel/Feuilleton* (Berlin), 25 August 1971, s. 4.

———. "Der Kanadische Realist." *Der Tagesspiegel/Feuilleton* (Berlin), 3 November 1971, s. 4.

Perkin, J.R.C. "Healing and Celebrating Art: An Introduction to Alex Colville." *The Second Mile* (Hantsport, NS) (February 1981): 3-8.

Perry, Arthur. "Increased Drama Shows in Colville's Latest Works." *The Vancouver Province*, 30 July 1977.

———. "Alex Colville's Art of the Seventies." *Artmagazine* 9 (March/April 1978): 42-43; 56.

Phillips, T.A. "Alex Colville." *Onion* 3 (October 1978): 6.

Porteous, John. "Alex Colville." *En Route* 8 (April 1980): 52-60; 70; 91.

Preston, Stuart. "Review, Hewitt Gallery." *New York Times*, 15 March 1953.

———. "Review, Hewitt Gallery." *New York Times*, 2 March 1955.

Primeau, Liz. "Painting it like it is." *Weekend Magazine* 23, 3 November 1973, p. 14.

Purdie, James. "Colville's Magic: He's Dangerously Close to God." *Globe and Mail* (Toronto), 26 November 1977, p. 33.

———. "Dazzling Challenge from Colville." *Globe and Mail* (Toronto), 9 September 1978, p. 35.

Redgrave, F. "The Season in Review–The Fourth Drawing Show at Dalhousie Art Gallery (1 March–1 April)." *Artmagazine* 43/44 (May/June 1979): 48-49.

Robertshaw, Ursula. "Magic Mirror." *Illustrated London News* 256, 31 January 1970, p. 26.

Robinson, Cyril. "Tails It's a Rabbit." *Weekend Magazine*, no. 1, 7 January 1967.

Russell, John. "Review." *Sunday Times* (London), 18 January 1970, p. 58.

Salvesen, C. "Drama?" *The Listener* (London), 29 January 1970.

Salvesen, Christopher. "Moments of Truth." *Montreal Star*, 28 March 1970. (Reprint of article in *The Listener*.)

Schreiber, Mathias. "Als guter Realist muss ich alles erfinden." *Kölner Stadt-Anzeiger*, 9 December 1971, s. 19.

Schröder, Thomas. "Bedrohliche Idyllen." *tween*, 13 Jahr, no. 4, 4 April 1971, s. 66-71.

Scott, Andrew. "Alex Colville Little Changed Since 1950s." *Performance*, 13-26 August 1977.

Sello, Gottfried. "Fopp-Art in Venedig." *Zeit Feuilleton*, no. 27, 1 Juli 1966, s. 20.

Sharp, Debra. "Attempt to Dramatize Work of Colville Works Well." *Globe and Mail* (Toronto), 20 June 1980. (Review of play by Theatre Passe Muraille, *Glazed Tempora*, based on Colville's paintings.)

Shaw, Avery. "Towards a Personal Realism," *Canadian Art*, 3 (Summer 1951): 164

Shepherd, Michael. "Alex Colville." *Arts Review* 22, 31 January 1970, p. 44.

Simpson, Anne. "An Artist in Canada: Alex Colville: The Brockington Visitor." *Queen's Journal*, 27 November 1981.

Sotriffer, Kristian. "Die Wahrheit oder die Freiheit." *Die Presse*. 3/4 February 1973, s. 17.

Stewart, Walter P. "An Appreciation of Alex Colville, Realist Painter." *Atlantic Advocate* 67 (November 1976): 9-10; 12.

Vaizey, Marina. "Alex Colville." *Arts Review*, 24 June 1977.

——. "Art." *Sunday Times* (London), 19 June 1977.

Wagner, Geoffrey. "Painting." *New Republic*, 12 July 1954.

EXHIBITIONS AND PUBLIC COLLECTIONS

GROUP SHOWS

1946   *RCA Exhibition*, Art Gallery of Toronto. Catalogue Raisonné No. 16.

1947   *Canadian Group of Painters*, Art Gallery of Toronto. Catalogue Raisonné No. 7; 19.

1950   *Canadian Group of Painters*, Art Gallery of Toronto. Catalogue Raisonné No. 22.

   11 New Brunswick Painters, Williams Memorial Art Museum, London, Ontario. Review: *London Evening Free Press*, 4 February 1950.

1952   *Group Show – Gallery Artists*, Hewitt Gallery, New York. Catalogue Raisonné No. 29. Review: *Art Digest*, 1 December 1952.

1954   *Reality and Fantasy 1900-1954*, Walker Art Center, Minneapolis. Catalogue Raisonné No. 29.

   Annual Art Exhibition, Montreal Museum of Fine Arts, Montreal. Catalogue Raisonné No. 36.

   64th Annual Exhibition of the Nebraska Art Association. Catalogue Raisonné No. 34.

   India, Pakistan and Ceylon. (Travelling Exhibition). Organized by the National Gallery of Canada. Catalogue Raisonné No. 34.

   Group Show – Gallery Artists, Hewitt Gallery, New York.

1955   *Five New Brunswick Artists*, Art Gallery of Toronto. Catalogue Raisonné No. 29; 32; 33; 34; 43; 46.

   International Exhibition of Painting, Venezuela. Catalogue Raisonné No. 47.

   1st Biennial Exhibition of Canadian Art, National Gallery of Canada, Ottawa. Catalogue Raisonné No. 30.

1956   *Canadian Society of Graphic Artists*, Art Gallery of Toronto. Catalogue Raisonné No. 123.

   Women's Committee Tenth Annual Sale of Art, Art Gallery of Toronto. Catalogue Raisonné No. 40.

   Tasmanian Museum and Art Gallery. Catalogue Raisonné No. 34.

   Ottawa Design Centre. Catalogue Raisonné No. 29.

1957   *2nd Biennial Exhibition of Canadian Art*, National Gallery of Canada, Ottawa. Catalogue Raisonné No. 53 (Award of Merit). Review: *Ottawa Citizen*, 30 March 1957.

   Women's Committee Eleventh Annual Sale of Art, Art Gallery of Toronto. Catalogue Raisonné No. 125.

   Calgary Jubilee Auditorium, Calgary, Alberta. Catalogue Raisonné No. 29.

1958   *First Inter-American Painting and Engraving Biennial Exhibition*, Mexico City. Catalogue Raisonné No. 56.

   Victoria Art Gallery Opening Exhibition. Victoria, BC. Catalogue Raisonné No. 30.

   The Winnipeg Art Gallery. Catalogue Raisonné No. 49.

   American Symbolic Realist Painters, Festival of Two Worlds. Spoleto, Italy.

   Canadian Pavilion Art Gallery, Brussels World's Fair. Catalogue Raisonné No. 29; 49.

   Centrall Museum der Gemeente, Utrecht, the Netherlands. Catalogue Raisonné No. 29; 49.

   Museum van Oudheden voor Provincie, Groningen, the Netherlands. Catalogue Raisonné No. 29; 49.

1959   *Zeitgenossische Kunst In Kanada*, Wallraf-Richartz. Museum, Köln, West Germany. Catalogue Raisonné No. 29; 49.

        Musée d'Art et d'Histoire, Geneva, Switzerland. Catalogue Raisonné No. 29; 49.

        Women's Committee Thirteenth Annual Sale of Art, Art Gallery of Toronto. Catalogue Raisonné No. 127.

        3rd Biennial Exhibition of Canadian Art, National Gallery of Canada, Ottawa. Catalogue Raisonné No. 55; 56.

        Stratford Shakespearean Festival. Catalogue Raisonné No. 53.

1960   Instituto National de Bellas Artes, Mexico. Catalogue Raisonné No. 56.

1961   *São Paulo Biennial Exhibition*, São Paulo, Brazil. Catalogue Raisonné No. 56.

        Women's Committee Art Sale, Art Gallery of Toronto. Catalogue Raisonné No. 128.

        The Group of Seven and After, Travelling Exhibition organized by the National Gallery of Canada, Ottawa. Catalogue Raisonné No. 31.

        London Public Library. (Travelling Exhibition), Catalogue Raisonné No. 34; 49; 53; 55.

1962   *Recent Canadian Painting*, Warsaw, Poland. Organized by the National Gallery of Canada. Catalogue Raisonné No. 37; 56; 60; 66.

        Commonwealth Art Today, Commonwealth Institute. London. Catalogue Raisonné No. 56.

1963   *Dunn International Exhibition*, Beaverbrook Art Gallery, Fredericton. Catalogue Raisonné No. 59, (Dunn International Award).

        Waterloo University. Waterloo, Ont. Catalogue Raisonné No. 31.

        The Lively Image, Art Institute of Ontario, Toronto. Catalogue Raisonné No. 31.

        The Museum of Modern Art, New York. Catalogue Raisonné No. 53.

1964   *Canadian Painting 1939-1963*, The Tate Gallery, London. Organized by the National Gallery of Canada. Catalogue Raisonné No. 27; 29; 45; 49; 55; 57; 58.

        Seventh Exhibition and Sale of Works by Canadian Artists, Musée des beaux-arts, Montreal. Catalogue Raisonné No. 71.

        The Magic of Realism, Banfer Gallery, New York. Catalogue Raisonné No. 72; 73.

1965   *The Magic of Realism*, Banfer Gallery, New York. Essay by Helen J. Dow.

        Art and Engineering, Art Gallery of Toronto. Catalogue Raisonné No. 66.

        Fourth Annual Festival of the Arts, McMaster University, Hamilton.

1966   *Canada 66*, XXXIII Venice Biennale Exhibition. Catalogue Raisonné No. 29; 55; 56; 58; 66; 67; 69; 70; 71; 72; 74; 129.

        Artists of Atlantic Canada, Atlantic Provinces Art Circuit. Catalogue Raisonné No. 22; 61; 63; 130.

1967   *Three Hundred Years of Canadian Art*, National Gallery of Canada, Ottawa. Catalogue Raisonné No. 44; 74.

        18 Canadian Artists, Norman Mackenzie Art Gallery. Regina, Saskatchewan. Catalogue Raisonné No. 73.

1968   *Nineteenth Annual Winter Exhibition*, Art Gallery of Hamilton. Catalogue Raisonné No. 77.

        Menschenbilder, Kunsthalle, Darmstadt. Catalogue Raisonné No. 75.

        Recent Acquisitions, Musée des beaux-arts, Montreal. Catalogue Raisonné No. 71.

1969   *Magic Realism in Canada*, University of Guelph, Guelph. Essay by Nancy-Lou Patterson. Catalogue Raisonné No. 49; 52; 53; 67.

1970   *Eight Artists From Canada*, Tel Aviv Museum, Tel Aviv, Israel. Catalogue Raisonné No. 29; 34; 49; 53; 55; 56; 58; 74.

1971   *Tenth Anniversary and Opening Ceremony for New Building Extension*, Sarnia Art Gallery. Catalogue Raisonné No. 29.

1972   *L'Art du XXe Siècle*, Musée des beaux-arts, Montreal. Catalogue Raisonné No. 71.

1974   *Masters of Graphic Art, Goya to Henry Moore*, Fischer Fine Art, London. Catalogue Raisonné No. 132; 134; 135.

        The Acute Image in Canadian Art, Owens Art Gallery, Mount Allison University, Sackville, NB. Catalogue Raisonné No. 43; 56; 71; 74; 86.

        Colville, Pratt and Forrestall, Beaverbrook Art Gallery, Fredericton, NB. Catalogue Raisonné No. 22; 24; 44; 59; 123; 128; 129; 131; 133; 134.

        Hyperréalistes Américains, Réalistes Européens, Centre nationale d'art contemporain, Paris. Catalogue Raisonné No. 55; 56; 60; 66; 69; 77; 78; 81; 83; 86; 88; 130; 131; 134.

        Paintings by Colville, Lichtenstein and Lindner, Fischer Fine Art, London. (Also shown in Stuttgart).

1975   *Realismus und Realität*, Kunsthalle, Darmstadt. Catalogue Raisonné No. 88; 91.

        The Ontario Community Collects, Art Gallery of Ontario, Toronto. Catalogue Raisonné No. 59.

1976   *Changing Visions: The Canadian Landscape*, Art Gallery of Ontario, Toronto. Catalogue Raisonné No. 52.

        Through Canadian Eyes: Trends and Influences in Canadian Art 1815-1965, Glenbow-Alberta Institute, Glenbow Centre, Calgary. Catalogue Raisonné No. 71.

1977   *Commonwealth Artists of Fame – 1952-1977*, Commonwealth Institute Art Gallery, London, England. Catalogue Raisonné No. 56; 135; 137.

1978   *The Work of Art: Six Artists*, Art Gallery of Ontario, Toronto. Catalogue Raisonné No. 86.

        Modern Painting in Canada, Edmonton Art Gallery. Catalogue Raisonné No. 49.

        The Image of Man in Canadian Painting, 1878-1978, McIntosh Art Gallery, London, Ont. Catalogue Raisonné No. 74.

        Coast, Sea and Canadian Art, The Gallery/Stratford, Ont. Catalogue Raisonné No. 55.

1980   *Annapolis Valley/Seven Artists*, Art Gallery of Nova Scotia, Halifax. Catalogue Raisonné No. 67; 71; 74; 113.

1981   *Canadian Artists of the Second World War*, The Robert McLaughlin Gallery, Oshawa. Essay by Joan Murray. Catalogue Raisonné No. 14; 15; 11.

        Twentieth Century Canadian Painting, National Museum of Modern Art, Tokyo. Catalogue Raisonné No. 29; 74.

1951   *Alex Colville*, New Brunswick Museum, Saint John. (Exhibition in conjunction with "Know Your Artists Series") Catalogue Raisonné No. 8; 14; 15; 16; 21; 22; 24; 25; 26; 27; 28. Reviews: *Evening Times Globe* (Saint John) 9 November 1951; *Daily News* (Amherst) 14 November 1951.

1953   *Alex Colville*, Hewitt Gallery, New York. Catalogue Raisonné No. 24; 26; 27; 29; 30; 31; 32; 33; 34. Reviews: *Art Digest*, 15 March 1955 (BH); *New York Herald Tribune*, 14 March 1955 (EG).

1955   *Alex Colville*, Hewitt Gallery, New York. Catalogue Raisonné No. 26; 31; 33; 35; 36; 37; 38; 39; 40; 41; 42; 43; 44; 45; 46; 47; 159.

1958   *Paintings by Alex Colville*, Laing Galleries. Toronto.

1963   *Alex Colville: Paintings*, Banfer Gallery, New York. Catalogue Raisonné No. 29; 31; 36; 39; 42; 45; 48; 52; 55; 57; 58; 59; 60; 61; 62; 63; 64; 65; 66; 67; 123; 124; 125; 126; 127; 128. Catalogue includes statement by the artist.

1966   *Alex Colville, 1944-46*, Travelling Exhibition of War Paintings, organized by the National Gallery of Canada, Ottawa.

        Magic Realism Paintings by Alex Colville, Hart House Gallery, University of Toronto. (Also shown at Laing Galleries, Toronto) Catalogue Raisonné No. 22; 24; 43; 48; 56; 57; 58; 71.

1969   *Katalog 7, Alex Colville*, Kestner-Gesellschaft, Hanover, West Germany. Catalogue Raisonné No. 55; 56; 58; 59; 60; 63; 65; 66; 67; 69; 70; 71; 72; 73; 74; 75; 76; 77; 78; 79; 80; 81; 128; 129; 130; 131; 132; 133.

1970   *Alex Colville*, Marlborough Fine Art, London. Catalogue Raisonné No. 55; 56; 58; 59; 60; 63; 65; 66; 67; 68; 69; 70; 71; 72; 73; 74; 75; 76; 77; 78; 79; 80; 81; 128; 129; 130; 131; 132; 133. Essay by Robert Melville. Reviews: *London City Press*, 20 January 1970; *Art & Antiques Weekly* (London), 17 January 1970; *The Times* (London), 3 February 1970; *Daily Telegraph* (London), 15 January 1970; *Evening Standard* (London), 20 January 1970; *Arts Review*, 17 January 1970; *The Tatler*, February 1970.

        Festival of Religion and the Arts: Work of Alex Colville, Student Union Art Gallery, University of Alberta, Edmonton. Catalogue Raisonné No. 42; 67; 126; 127; 128; 129; 130; 131; 132; 133; 150.

1971   *Alex Colville Serigraphies*, Université de Moncton: Galerie d'art. Moncton, NB. Catalogue Raisonné No. 123; 124; 125; 126; 127; 128; 129; 130; 131; 132; 133; 134.

1972   Moose Jaw Museum, Moose Jaw, Sask. Catalogue Raisonné No. 53 (Indefinite loan).

1974   *Alex Colville: Collection of Helen J. Dow*, McLaughlin Library, University of Guelph. Catalogue Raisonné No. 23; 42; 61; 67; 126; 127; 128; 129; 130; 131; 132; 133; 134; 135; 136; 147; 150.

1975   *Alex Colville: Labours of the Months*, Downstairs Gallery, Edmonton. Catalogue Raisonné No. 92-103 (inc.).

1976   *Alex Colville*, Norman Mackenzie Art Gallery, Regina, Saskatchewan. Catalogue Raisonne No. 24; 29; 42; 43; 44; 53; 54; 56; 60; 61; 67; 70; 74; 86; 88.

        Picture of the Month, Confederation Centre Art Gallery, Charlottetown, PEI. Catalogue Raisonné No. 74.

1977   *Alex Colville: Paintings and Drawings (1970-1977)*, Kunsthalle, Düsseldorf and Fischer Fine Art, London. Catalogue Raisonné No. 82; 83; 84; 85; 86; 87; 88; 90; 91; 92-103 (inc.); 104; 105; 106; 107; 108; 109; 110; 134; 135; 136; 137; 147; 148.

   Alex Colville – Galerie Royale, Vancouver (From Fischer Show).

1978   *Alex Colville*, Mira Godard Gallery. Toronto and Montreal. Catalogue Raisonné No. 78; 86; 88; 107; 109; 110; 112; 113.

1981   *Alex Colville: War Artist*, (Travelling Exhibition) Organized by the Canadian War Museum, Ottawa (40 works) Catalogue Raisonné No. 3; 12; Review: *Hamilton Spectator*, 28 November 1981; *Charlottetown Guardian*, 22 February 1982.

PUBLIC COLLECTIONS

New Brunswick Museum, Saint John

National Gallery of Canada, Ottawa

Art Gallery of Hamilton

Art Gallery of Ontario, Toronto

Musée des beaux-arts, Montreal

The Museum of Modern Art, New York

Museum Ludwig, Cologne

Kestner-Gesellschaft, Hanover

Nationalgalerie, East Berlin

Musée national d'art moderne
   Centre Georges Pompidou, Paris

Museum Boymans-van Beuningen,
   Rotterdam

Museum der moderner Kunst, Vienna

Kitchener-Waterloo Art Gallery, Kitchener

Beaverbrook Art Gallery, Fredericton

Lynnwood Arts Centre, Simcoe

London Regional Art Gallery, London, Ont.

Mendel Art Gallery, Saskatoon

Vancouver Art Gallery, Vancouver

BIOGRAPHICAL CHRONOLOGY

1920	David Alexander Colville born 24 August, Toronto. Second son of David Harrower Colville and Florence Gault Colville. One brother, Robert Colville 1915-1976. Moved to St. Catharines, Ontario, 1927, then Amherst, Nova Scotia, 1929.
1942	BFA, Mount Allison University, Sackville, New Brunswick.
	Entered Canadian Army.
	Married Rhoda Wright, Wolfville, Nova Scotia, 5 August.
1943	Received commission in Canadian Army, 11 September.
1944	Sent overseas as War Artist, May.
	Birth of first son, Graham, 15 July.
1945	Returned to Canada, October. Completed service as war artist in Ottawa.
1946	Demobilized from army, June.
	Began teaching at Mount Allison University, Sackville.
	Birth of second son, John, 26 July.
1948	Birth of third son, Charles, 15 February.
1949	Birth of daughter, Ann, 6 August.
1951	First one-man exhibition, New Brunswick Museum, Saint John.
1953	First one-man exhibition in the US, Hewitt Gallery, New York.
1955	Second one-man exhibition, Hewitt Gallery, New York.
1958	Exhibition, Laing Galleries, Toronto, and Hart House, University of Toronto.
1963	Won Dunn International Award, Beaverbrook Art Gallery, Fredericton, NB (Catalogue Raisonné No. 58).
	Exhibition, Banfer Gallery, New York.
	Resigned from Mount Allison University to devote himself full-time to his art.
1965	Awarded commission from Canadian Government to design coins commemorating Canada's Centennial Year.
	Led a Painting and Drawing Workshop, University of Alberta, Edmonton.
1966	Represented Canada at XXXIII Venice Biennale Exhibition.
1967	Officer of Order of Canada.
	Honorary Degree, (D.Litt.), Trent University, Peterborough, Ontario.
1967/68	Visiting artist, University of California at Santa Cruz.
1968	Honorary Degree, (LLD), Mount Allison University, Sackville.
1969	Exhibition, Kestner-Gesellschaft, Hanover, West Germany.
	Honorary Degree, (LLD), Dalhousie University, Halifax, Nova Scotia.
1970	Exhibition, Marlborough Fine Art Gallery, London, England.
1971	Visiting artist, Berliner Kunstlerprogramm.

1973   Moved from Sackville, New Brunswick to present home in Wolfville, Nova Scotia.

Honorary Degree, (LLD), Simon Fraser University, Vancouver, British Columbia.

Honorary Degree, (LLD), University of Windsor, Windsor, Ontario.

1975   Awarded Molson Prize, Canada Council.

Honorary Degree, (D.Litt.), Acadia University, Wolfville, Nova Scotia.

1976   Exhibition, Norman Mackenzie Art Gallery, Regina, Saskatchewan.

1977   Exhibitions, Gemeentmuseum, Arnhem; Kunsthalle, Düsseldorf; Fischer Fine Art, London.

1978   Designed Medal for Governor General and Mrs. Jules Léger.

Exhibitions, Mira Godard Gallery, Toronto and Montreal.

1981   Appointed Chancellor, Acadia University, Wolfville, Nova Scotia.

Brockington Lecturer, Queen's University, Kingston, Ontario.

Honorary Degree, (D.Litt.), Memorial University, St. John's, Newfoundland.

1982   Companion of the Order of Canada.

Lives and works in Wolfville, Nova Scotia.

INDEX